CW01019925

NIKKI

...all about secrets

NIKKI

...all about secrets

NICK CHARLES

as told to him by

Nikki de Villiers

GARRICK HOUSE

Published 2003 by Garrick House Ltd
Reg No. 3555559
Victoria Road, Diss, Norfolk IP22 4JG

ISBN 1-902573-03-X

Copyright © 2003 Nick Charles

The right of Nick Charles to be identified as author of this
work has been asserted by him in accordance with the
Copyright, Designs and Patents Act 1988.

A CIP catalogue record for this book is available from the
British Library.

Cover design © Oakwood 2002
Printed and bound in Great Britain by
Creative Print and Design (Wales) Ebbw Vale

1 3 5 7 9 8 6 4 2

CONTENTS

Page No:

Chapter

We have escaped like a bird from the hunter's
trap;
The trap is broken and we are free!

Psalm 124 v 7

Some names have been changed, to protect the guilty and innocent alike.

DEDICATION

TO CHARLOTTE
MY CAVALIER KING CHARLES SPANIEL

WHO WAS FIRST TO REALLY LOVE ME

TO
SALLY
WHO IS HAYLEY
WHO IS ME

and

TO THE MEMORY OF
MY BELOVED
MISS KATHLEEN LEWIS

ACKNOWLEDGEMENT

A huge thank you to Nick Charles for everything he has done for me in my new sober life, including writing this book which has been a difficult venture for both of us.

I would like to acknowledge the few people along the way who did try to help me and failed through no fault of theirs.

Finally, my sincere thanks for the support I have received from all my friends who have made my new life worth living.

NIKKI de VILLIERS

INTRODUCTION by Nick Charles

When my autobiography "Through A Glass Brightly" was published in November 1998, I was convinced it contained all the hell on earth I was likely to encounter in my lifetime. This assumption was about to change.

I was enjoying my customary Friday night non-alcoholic evening with Chaucer Clinic's General Manager Nikki de Villiers, when the conversation took a sinister turn. I had spent the early years of our relationship counselling her for anorexia nervosa, alcohol addiction, drug abuse and self-body mutilation. She had severe psychiatric problems, which manifested themselves predominately through an acute hatred for herself, and a masochistic compulsion to damage her body in any way she could.

Her anorexia presented an entirely separate set of problems. Quite apart from the symptoms well documented on this awful condition, she was a heavy smoker and coupled with lack of food, her circulatory system was breaking down. Her GP informed me that, should she continue alcoholic drinking and anorexic behaviour, it was almost certain that gangrene would develop in one particular limb, and an amputation become inevitable.

The origin of these horrendous manifestations were rooted in a physically and sexually abused childhood. It was a question that came out of the blue during a normally predictable Friday evening and would change my life and thinking in a way I could never have imagined. Suddenly she asked.

'Do you actually understand the nature of child sexual abuse and the shape it takes?' Nikki's eyes were levelled steadily at mine and her eyelids and gaze stayed firm.

Suddenly I realised how vital it was, particularly for a counsellor in my position, to be made aware precisely of what the actual physical and emotional process of the perpetrator's actions entailed. I admitted to her I did not know everything, but was prepared to listen.

Nikki proceeded to open a door to an evil in our society of epidemic proportions with descriptions of abuse two years of intense therapy had failed to uncover. She explained that far from being distinguishable by their sinister appearance, abusers are far more likely to be the nice guy next door. A relative, a teacher, the priest or those in responsible positions of trust and respectability. Typically, the victims are in their thirties or forties before they summon up the courage to talk. Many by this time are irreparably damaged, yet incredibly a sizeable proportion do not harbour any hatred towards their abusers. Such is the disguised pleasure they bring, so insidious is the clever build-up by the apparently loving and caring attacker, that a common emotion despite the terrible damage and trauma caused, is acceptance of that which cannot be changed and often an inability to hate or even dislike their tormentors.

It was a story that Nikki wanted to tell explicitly and I felt had to be told. I asked myself a thousand times if I had the courage to write it, and my decision swung backwards and forwards like the pendulum of a clock.

Finally it stopped and I put pen to paper. In this introduction words would prove woefully inadequate to prepare the reader for the horrors they are about to encounter. To make it clear this is not an historical document of a never-to-be-repeated one-off life, is vital. As you read these words, a child - perhaps next door to where you live - could be a victim. I hope with every ounce of decency in my body that the following pages strike a mighty blow for children who have lost, or who are currently losing their childhoods because of an evil that defies description.

PREFACE

Nikki de Villiers was the Chaucer Clinic's first patient. At first her progress was slow, one step forward and more often two backwards, there seemed little hope of any chance of a normal existence. No-one could have conceived the extent of the damage to which she had been exposed, until they entered her world.

In the beginning she was difficult to get to know, and suspicious of those around her. She was easily intimidated and appeared threatened by health professionals, all those who tried to help her expected a long job.

No-one could have possibly foreseen the sequence of events about to unfold, but amazing stories are born out of nightmares.

Life became a constant daily battle in recovery, as she was torn between one hour of normality and twenty three hours of torment. One good hour became two, became four as the months went by and then miraculously her first anniversary of sobriety which included twelve months of substantially less self-mutilation and almost full-time eating.

Nikki's first job at Chaucer Clinic was toilet cleaner, and she mopped out the stone floored corridors with mop and bucket twice daily. At night she sweated through unending hallucinations and relived the evils of an horrendously abused child-hood, and formative years that trod a similar road.

In June 1990 she began counselling other admissions and in 1991 became Assistant Manager. In 1993 she reached the dizzy heights of General Manager of Britain's biggest, alcohol rehabilitation clinic and in the latter part of that year became the proud owner of her own home. In January 2001, Nikki reached out to millions on the World Wide Web. She became Agony Aunt on www.addictionnetwork.co.uk, one of the busiest addiction websites in the world ~ her friends and workmates had witnessed a modern day miracle.

She has such a depth of experience from her life she is able to offer counselling on a wide vari-ety of issues. She has endured a childhood of abuse, childrens' homes, fostering, disruption and the distress of being torn between two families. Her teenage years were filled with problems including an unplanned pregnancy, an alcoholic marriage, subsequent divorce, homelessness, mental and physical abuse, rape and murder.

During her life she has had to come to terms with events and experiences far beyond most peo-ple's comprehension. The resulting alcoholism, anorexia and self-mutilation were the only way she knew of coping with the memories and horrors of her life.

In sobriety Nikki has found a way to live in the real world of work, relationships, emotions, and day-to-day routine, without the anaesthetic of alcohol.

She is an exceptional lady with unique qualifications, whose greatest wish is to share her way to recovery with others affected by alcoholism and a wide range of other problems. Her story opens on the eve of her tenth anniversary of a life alcohol free. On the recommendation of her counsellor, she is revisiting the city of her birth and the scene of her suffering. There were many skeletons to bury, many ghosts to lay and a psychological barrier that had to be broken down.

Few victims would want to take part in an exercise of their private hell revisited - onlookers might be intrigued by the journey if they could make it as a silent witness.....

The reader is invited to experience both.

CHAPTER ONE

PITY MY SIMPLICITY

Andante
(slowly with feeling)

I sat on a wooden bench in the city centre of one of the most beautiful parts of England enjoying the summer sunshine, and watched myself get chatted up by the boys. Well! Sort of ...

I had returned to my home town to lay a few ghosts, try and take stock and face the last few demons in my soul. My day had begun at Braunton House. I had sat outside for an hour remembering times long ago that had shaped my life. The building looked completely innocuous with ivy growing up the sides and a garden full of colour.

My memories were more sinister. The rules had been strict, I was made to eat food I hated at times when I wasn't hungry, and I was not allowed to be with my brother and sisters. My poor mother had taken one beating too many from our father, and dumped all five of us on a desk at the social services department. Braunton House was the local children's home.

I had sobbed until there were no more tears and found I could cope if I rocked backwards and forwards...incessantly. I withdrew into a private world where I didn't have to speak and pretended to read books from a big pile and play with mainly broken toys that other kids came and took away from me.

More than anything I longed for my mummy to be with me and love me, or at the very least for someone to come and hold me tightly. Sometimes it would become a dream. One night my dream came true.

It was night-time, I had been asleep and the lady who worked the evenings was shaking my shoulder gently.

'Come on luvvy, I'm going to tell you a story.' She picked me up and held me tightly kissing my cheek and I remember the sheer pleasure as if it was only yesterday. She carried me to a room I recall as being white and clinical and sat me on a bed-like couch and smoothed my hair lovingly. She lifted my nightie over my head and laid me down full length on the white sheeted surface, then went over to a row of cupboards and returned with a small jar. I watched her intently as she unscrewed the top and scooped out something yellow on her fingers. Slowly she smoothed the soft pleasant smelling cream into my skin, starting at my chest and working her way down until she arrived at my tummy. I felt her fingers penetrate between my thighs and I opened my legs wider because I remembered it was more enjoyable that way. Daddy's finger had felt bigger. He had only done it in the bath and sometimes for so long the water got cold. The lady was more gentle and asked me if it was nice, I didn't say but hoped she would not stop. I waited for her to get pretending rough with me like Daddy did. He would smack my bottom then kiss it better and then put his finger back inside me again; she did not. Her hands would gently smooth around the area Mummy called my wee-wee and keep adding the cream that smelled so beautiful. All the time she spoke gentle words, I do not remember any of them only that they were loving, almost as loving as her fingers probing my most tender parts. I didn't want it to end, but suddenly she stopped and said. 'My turn now!'

She stood up and began undoing the buttons on her housecoat starting at the top. When she arrived halfway she slipped it from her shoulders, sat down and removed her bra revealing very large breasts, much larger than my mummy's. She put some yellow cream on each side, asked me to rub it in, I made a mess, she tutted, I thought she didn't love me anymore and cried.

'Well do I get a ride then?'

The voice in my memory brought me back from childlike thinking to the present and my attention reverted to watching the antics across the city street of the girl who was me with a boy in a sports car.

I felt the ire rise under the collar of my cotton top as my brain went into adult mode away from the infant state, and I gritted my teeth.

The sports car was yellow, Japanese, sleek and fast looking. I looked back at she who was me, long blonde hair, probably bleached although more professionally than mine had been at the same age, and decided to give her a new name that was old... Hayley, I would call her Hayley.

Hayley flirted shamelessly across the street, chip off the old block, skirt nine inches above the knee, I already knew her knickers were white. Had she been spared a childhood like mine?

I relaxed as my anger ebbed away, yet inexplicably I let my memory wander back to the clinical white room of my world when I was four years old, and the interruption I remembered from all those years ago.

'Hello Joan.' The voice was like I imagined Billy Goat Gruff to be and 'large breasts' swung freely in the direction of the voice.

I jumped in surprise at his sudden arrival, the lady who loved me stood up abruptly and ran to his arms. They hugged and kissed and wrestled in a way my mother and father had never done, I felt deserted, forgotten, unloved..... suddenly I caught his attention. He walked towards me in silence and laid me back down on the couch and gently stroked between my legs. I felt a finger, bigger even than Daddy's had been, slip deep inside me and slide backwards and forwards slowly and wonderfully, I closed my eyes and drifted into wonderland. He obviously loved me too.

'I'm your Auntie Joan's friend.' His voice was loud and gruff, though not unfriendly, and when he had taken off his clothes I noticed he was covered in hair. I realised he loved Auntie Joan as well as me, because she joined us on the couch and we all three sat together caressing and playing little games. Billy Gruff had something like one of Mummy's rolling pins, but not quite so large, sticking out below his tummy. He moved closer to Auntie Joan and I watched enthralled as it disappeared slowly inside her. She changed immediately. She didn't love Billy Gruff anymore, they fought all over the floor and both screamed at each other. I cried more than ever before in fear of her being hurt and in sorrow that their love was ended. Suddenly, the shouting stopped and they stood up and returned to the couch-cum-bed and lay by my side. I was confused. Auntie Joan held Billy Gruff's rolling pin and shook it. It suddenly leaked a milky cream and the shouting started again; I was aware of his closeness to me and the warm liquid cascading over my face and body. Then I realised how important I was to them, they turned towards me together and rubbed the sticky unguent gently into my skin. Then followed bathtime, my second of the evening, my nightie was replaced and back to my bed, I felt warmth and happiness for the love I had enjoyed, and finally a rare untroubled sleep.

The days were long and boring. Occasionally I would see Auntie Joan during the day, but she never recognised me even though on several occasions I stood right in front of her as she passed by.

She only came to me at night-time and almost always with Billy Goat Gruff. We would invariably play the same wonderful games with incredible sensations that made my body tremble, and each day I would long for the night.

Now and again I would be disappointed. I would sit in the corner alone where they had put me, they did not want me or had forgotten I was there, or perhaps they did not love me anymore. Then, just as I was lost in my sorrow, hurt and misery, they would gently remove my night clothes and rub their fingers lightly over the whole of my body with the delicious yellow cream.

Then one day something terrible happened. I had not seen my brother for weeks but suddenly we were together, dressed in crisp, clean clothes.

'We have a lovely new home for you both to go to, with a new mummy and daddy.' I was bewildered and my head swam deliriously with thoughts of misery of a life without Auntie Joan and Billy Goat Gruff. The man who made the announcement was red faced, fat and held a large book under his arm, and he smiled comically like Humpty Dumpty.

We were taken to Humpty's car. My brother Roy walked, I was half carried half dragged and screamed blue murder throughout the journey. On arrival 'new' mummy and daddy welcomed us with two children of their own. I recall them doing the best they could to placate me, but I cried non-stop throughout the evening, all night and the following day. Within twenty four hours I was back at

Braunton House, but Roy liked it and stayed.

They tried to place me with well-meaning families several times after that, but I just wanted to be back with Auntie Joan and Billy Gruff. To them I was special, they loved me and I loved them with all my heart. Of course, I knew that nothing lasted for very long, and one day I realised there had only been Auntie Joan and I for quite some time. Shortly afterwards a new lady appeared in the evening and although I followed her around, she kept putting me back to bed. I wanted her to love me too, she was very nice and kind, but bath-time was very different and when we had fun all the kids joined in. Without having someone to love me I began to withdraw even more into my silent world. One day a man and a lady came to see me and asked if I would like to go and visit a new home. I nodded. When I arrived the first thing I saw was a cat - I had always wanted a cat - I never wanted to leave, ever again.

My new parents were Mr. and Mrs. Barker. They had a daughter four years my senior, called Felicity, who tried from the beginning to make me feel as welcome as her mother and father undoubtedly did. Trouble was, none of them knew where I'd been. I knew from the beginning they did not love me. Bathtime was soapsuds and floating ducks but nothing that felt nice. Bedtime was all in one place, and a story, and a kiss on the fore-head - I screamed for more. Mrs. Barker sat on the side of my bed and did nothing, even though I pushed the bedclothes down and pulled my nightie up. She did cuddle me and hold me tight, I liked that, it stopped me crying. When she gently let me down onto the bed so I could be left to sleep, I would wake and scream for her return. I cannot remember for sure, but I think it went on for months.

Slowly I got used to the routine, although it was not like the home I had shared with my real mum and dad before the children's home. Mrs. Barker had a washing machine, I told her my mother did not. She had a vacuum cleaner, I told her my mum had to use a brush and pan. I said, 'We never had a fridge.' Almost every day during the first few months I would make observations, tell her how happy we had always been - 'My mummy was a super cook.'

Eventually I settled into the peaceful routine of a middle class suburban homelife. After a few weeks Mrs. Barker asked if I would like her to be my new mum and Mr. Barker my dad. I said I already had a mum and dad, Felicity said I could be her sister, I was confused, you see for private reasons I knew none of them really loved me.

'See ya later, 'bout seven, don't forget you're staying at my house and me at yours,' Hayley's game with 'sports car boy' and the others was over, now she was off home to prepare for the night - I had returned swiftly back to the present, but soon drifted back to the past.

When barely seven years of age I had given my new mum a scare. I went missing, only for a couple of hours, I had gone to see Auntie Joan and

Billy Goat Gruff, but they were nowhere to be found. The anger was rising again. If I could put my hands around their throats now, I would squeeze the life out of them. The anger receded yet again, just like it always did because I remembered it had given me pleasure at the time. Why had they chosen me from a home full of children? Perhaps I had done something to encourage them. I had three other sisters yet my real father had only picked on me for special attention. I must have been to blame.

It was good in many ways to be back in my home town. I had already remade some old friendships and retraced footsteps. I was aware an urge had returned and I needed a drink, instead I thought of incredible experiences that had shaped my life and decided against. I walked sixty or seventy yards to the best hotel in town where I had once worked as a barmaid but was now arriving as a patron. At the reception desk I confirmed my reservation and was escorted by an immaculately uniformed porter to one of their most expensive suites. I handed him a gratuity that was probably double the wage they had paid me for a week in the days when I would have been his colleague, and lowered my eyes almost regally as he offered profuse thanks.

I knew people who had kept a packet of cigarettes in a secret place long after they had given up smoking. I rifled in the bottom of my handbag and felt an overwhelming inexplicable relief when I found an unopened plastic container of Wilkinson

Sword razor blades. I sat on the edge of the bed and fantasised at the pleasure I would experience if I were to cut a vein and watch as the escaping blood drained from me. I put the blades back into the bag and closed it...hard!

I undressed slowly and stood in the shower for much longer than necessary, then I dressed carefully in a black trouser suit with a faint executive stripe and planned my night. Finally, I checked my make-up yet again, took a final twirl in front of the full length mirror, and headed for the bar. My plan for the first night was simple. I was forty, looked thirty with a figure most women of my age would die for. The hotel was full of executive high flyers from several major companies, and one of them was going to have his tongue hanging out all night - and all for absolutely nothing. I had worked out every last detail, as near I could of course. There must be no possible risk to life or limb, and I would not stray from the hotel, my buzz was simply that I would pretend to be a thoroughly respectable and decent female. I never had one night stands!!

He transpired to be in a group of six. All early forties, all handsome in different ways, all well off and probably married. I was not the only woman available, there were several in fact, but I knew I had that certain 'je ne sais quoi' so indefinable to the male species who lived forever under its spell. I had carefully scrutinised the other females; the night was mine. There was nothing sinister about my actions, it was just that I had never had a platonic night out with a member of the opposite sex, tonight I wanted to know what it was like, to enjoy male company no strings attached. He would not know naturally, and I had, somehow, to play the part of the sophisticated lady whose last thought was a romp in the sack when this would be his only thought. As soon as it became obvious that my attention was dominated by Cornelius, one by one the others drifted away. I felt my cheeks burning and was relieved they went pink not red as I forced myself not to dwell on his name. I wondered if it was ever shortened. Lius had a ring about it - Con was O.K. - the thought of Corn, Corny or Neli made it hard to stay straight faced. I waited for the usual confessions that made the way clear for the inevitable pull. 'My wife doesn't understand me!' 'We have an open marriage.' 'We sleep in separate rooms.' Instead he invited me to join him for dinner. I was certainly not a man-hater and he seemed an extremely nice person, so I thought I'd offer him the bad news first.

'I'm in a permanent relationship so there will be nothing other than a pleasant evening in it for you Cornelius.' I bit my lip hard as I said his name whilst conveying the news. He didn't just look hurt, he actually looked mortified!

'I really had no such aspersions.' For a moment he played with the handle of his half pint glass and lowered his eyes, and after he said 'aspersions' I thought of nasturtiums in the silence that followed. Paradoxically, I was halfway amused at my lack of education and the fact that I owned a top of the range sports car and a luxury flat. I was General Manager at my place of work, yet had become sub-normal during the years of my illness. Auntie Joan had a lot to answer for. My brain and thinking often raced out of control, and I had many times planned exactly how I would murder Billy Goat Gruff.

'Oh! C'mon Cornelius, we'll go Dutch.' I grabbed him by the sleeve and we headed towards the restaurant.

He was a lovely man. Given another chance at the 'Great Plan' I might have settled for him, and my thoughts wandered to things that might have been. I discovered he was thirty eight, Managing Director of an electronic component manufacturing company, and unmarried. He described the only woman he had ever loved so intricately, I quickly felt I knew her intimately and even felt a personal loss at the news of her sudden death in a road accident. He had been unable to form any sort of permanent relationship since and had no desire to do so. There was a long silence when he had done, he saw his life as destroyed and I thought that, though terribly sad, he almost wallowed in it - I told him so. He was angry at first, but I went into therapy mode at which I excelled, I could almost see the lines on his forehead even out with relief as he unloaded. I expected no less of myself, I was good at my job and smiled at the irony that I was probably paid more to do it than Cornelius received for being a Managing Director. Despite the fact he cried a lot and we drew a few odd looks from other diners, they were silent tears and our voices low, he had told his story unashamedly and noticed no-one around him. Oddly, we both enjoyed the evening. Me for reasons of my own, he, because it had closed the last page in the final chapter of his own personal nightmare.

I had become accustomed to the fact a good time would never ever be the same again. Once I had taken my last alcoholic drink I soon realised the incredible depth of friendship, the amazing beauty in romances, in fact the unbelievable intensity of all my experiences, were inspired by alcohol and could never be repeated unless...! I shuddered. It must never happen again.

Cornelius thanked me profusely and towards the end a little drunkenly, but when I finally placed my head on the hotels luxury pillow alone in my suite, I was at peace with myself.

Was it possible I was beginning to like me?

CHAPTER TWO

THE GREAT ESCAPE

I lay there for a long time without sleep. My mind was preoccupied with my first two years with the Barkers and how hard they had tried to make me one of their family.

It was certainly not without upheavals, not the least of which was the strange attitude and unpredictable mood swings of this child to whom they had elected to offer a home. They had no inkling of the trauma created by the instability and confusion of believing love was one thing, only to discover it was something entirely different - or was it? All this in the mind of a seven year old child who translated it into sullen bewilderment through a misunderstood disposition, which was all she could show to the world. I thought of Felicity and recognised how hard she had tried, I could also see why she had given up and surrendered any hope of being a sister to this awful child. It was not hard for her to show how much she hated me, nor why she continues to do so to this very day.

I pondered on the social services enquiries that the family had undergone to establish their suitability. It must have been embarrassing, but not nearly so as that which I endured when, once a year, I had to strip naked and walk up and down in front of three men whom I did not know. By all accounts one was a doctor and the others apparently two experts of some sort who could tell from what they saw whether I was being abused or not. In addition, once or twice a year I had to meet up with my real family in order to maintain a family link. I had absolutely nothing to say to them - all it did was tear one half of me one way and the other half the other. Felicity did not know of this, nor did she ever know how much I loved her and wished that she and her parents could be my only family. Interestingly, Mandy, my middle sister who was the more mature of the five of us (though I was hardly capable at seven of major decision making) was determined enough to rebel at the bizarre rituals and make a stand. I never saw her again and learned in later life she had chosen to become adopted together with my brother Roy. We all had the choice of course, but mine came later when I was eleven.

My experiences at Braunton House and those previously with my real father, had occurred several times a week for the first five years of my life. It took time and a deal of confusion to consider that this was, perhaps, not the norm. Anyway if it wasn't some of it had to have been my fault. One day something happened that would begin to shape my perception of normal and acceptable, and of wrong and unacceptable.

'Would you like to go to live in Singapore?' My foster mother had sat Felicity and myself down on the settee in the front room and the question hung in the air like smoke from a cigarette.

'Where's Singapore?' It was me who had broken the silence imagining a fourpenny bus ride, and my foster father was ready with the answer. By the side of his chair lay a large book, and it took both his strong arms to lift it up on to the coffee table that stood in the middle of the floor.

'This,' he announced, 'is a World Atlas.' A small piece of white paper marked the spot and we all pored over the lilac, green and yellow coloured lined shapes that meant precious little to me and only a shade more to Felicity.

'There's a slender stick of land south of Thailand that stretches down to Malaya west of the South China Sea.' Dad sounded confident and accomplished in his knowledge. 'And, at the southernmost tip, is Singapore." He stood up and puffed out his chest in triumph. 'If we go it means a big promotion for me at work.' He sat back down and the previous silence continued.

'We'll go by plane,' offered Mum hopefully.

'What about all my friends? I've just started at my senior school.' Felicity looked as if she might cry.

'What's going to happen to the cat?' I almost screamed the last word, I had only come to live with them because they had a cat. Mother answered me. 'Mrs. Evans next door will have him until we come back.' 'Will we have a cat when we get there?' My voice was relentless. 'No, but you can have a monkey.' Dad's eyes twinkled. He would be long dead before I truly appreciated his sense of humour. 'Why can't I have a cat?' I was sounding desperate. 'Because it's a different culture, they do things differently.' His eyes were twinkling again and he said. 'The Chinese eat anything with four legs except a table - and anything that flies except a kite, so you can't have a cat.'

I froze in horror at the very thought of cat or dog for dinner, Felicity did the same for reasons of her own and the twinkle had gone from Dad's eye. Mum was beginning to look desperate but she took temporary control. 'Look, let's leave it for now, there is a great deal to be discussed and decided upon before we can make a definite decision.' Felicity and I were glad, perhaps Singapore would go away.

It did not go away, and three months later we were climbing aboard an east bound jet to begin a new life...eight thousand miles from home. Twenty five years later I would learn that the whole thing was nearly called off due to the ramifications of taking a foster child out of the country. The passage of time has done nothing to stop me crying every time I think of the fact that they wanted me more than the Singapore trip, which went far to set them up financially for life. If only I had known how vitally important I was to them at the time. If only!

Despite my tender years there was much I remembered about the first hours in our new country. Felicity crying uncontrollably when the plane doors opened and the humidity and an awful smell hit us. The hustle and bustle and the indecipherable chatter - the fuss created by me having a different surname to the Barkers on my passport, but mainly the smell. It was a mixture of fetid food, humidity (90'ish), smelly bodies, and.... God only knows what else! I went, 'Pooh!' Felicity just cried.

Despite all, I had many wonderful memories. Singaporeans laughed a lot and I learnt to swim like a fish. Their island is about the size of the Isle of Wight and the naval base, where Dad was going to work, was roughly where Cowes is, covering an area of about ten square miles. Much of my knowledge came later from long conversations with my mum, and also when an amazing coincidence in my thirties introduced me to a psychiatrist, Dr. David Marjot at my place of work, who had been serving at the British Military Hospital in Singapore at the same time we were there.

He would go to enormous lengths to answer my tiresome questions and describe the amazing changes that have taken place since. I remembered my father telling me stories of the naval barracks with a wonderful and unforgettable name - 'H.M.S. Terror' - about the dockyard and the Malayan navy's base that employed around thirty thousand men and had a dry dock capable of accommodating the largest ships afloat.

Singapore City was about fifteen miles away where Ventnor would be if you used my example of the Isle of Wight. It was a thriving city of eleven or twelve million people, mostly Chinese but with Malays and Indians too, that became independent in 1967. I recall, when an employee of the U.K government first came to Singapore they nearly always had to live in private accommodation as there was not enough housing in or near the navy or airforce bases. After a year or two they would be able to move into 'married quarters'.

Most of the army bases were in Singapore City. There were also army schools staffed by civilians. I went to Pasir Panjang School and have a wonderful mural of it on my bedroom wall that I commissioned an artist friend to copy from an old school magazine.

I clearly remember one very exciting time. In 1965 the Indonesians under Sukhano tried to seize Singapore by an internal uprising, mainly by the Malays and Communist element. There was a lot of shooting and what seemed flashing lights and explosions. There was a curfew that lasted many months and schooling was suspended - I spent almost the entire time in the swimming pool. Even to this day I can swim like a fish.

Each of the armed services bases were a community with its own facilities including swimming pools. Leisure life revolved around swimming pools, literally. The temperature never fell below 90oF with humidity at 95 %. It was very hot and sticky. Providing you were fit and acclimatised it was tolerable. I was very young, in paradise and loved every second. I do remember the rainy seasons and laugh quietly when I hear folk in the U.K. complain of torrential rain. Rain! They have never seen it. On both sides of every road were deep trench-like dykes and during the rainy season they carried rainwater in torrents. Imagine the worst possible rain we ever get in the U.K., even if only for a few seconds, now imagine that lasting for maybe six weeks without stopping - then you have the rains of Singapore.

Everyone had an 'Amah' (servant) who did the washing, cleaning and some cooking. If you could afford it you also had a cook or cook-boy - we had Emmy....she was lovely. The airforce was at Seletar and Changi where the infamous prison was and still is. Changi had a super side. There was a lovely club and swimming pool and I recall once swimming there during a monsoon that hammered down so hard the rain stung my shoulders and back even through the water.

My first history lesson at Pasir Panjang School stands out as if yesterday. The teacher held a cane and smiled, a contradiction that startled me at first. She had a sing-song voice that made her words live on for a lifetime.

'When Sir Stamford Raffles sailed into Sinagapore in 1819,' she sang beautifully, 'he brought with him an entourage of one hundred and twenty Indian assistants and soldiers. These were probably the first Indian settlers on the island, they resided mainly near Chulia Street which is in Chinatown, a place Raffles had originally designated for his Indian helpers. In the late nineteenth century many more Indian migrants arrived to work, usually building roads, clearing swamps or in civil service positions.

'The main reasons for the influx of Indians to the area known today as Little India was the introduction of cattle-rearing on the extremely fertile land near Rocher River. In addition, the building of the race course for the Europeans in 1843. Immigrants from Calcutta, Madras and Malaya flocked here and by the turn of the century this once plantation area covered by gambier, banana and vegetables, had become a flourishing commercial centre for the Indian community. It spread from both sides of Sarangoon Road and became known affectionately as Little India.'

'Ms. de Villiers, Ms. de Villiers, your eight o'clock call!'

I jumped out of the South China Sea and landed back on my hotel bed.

CHAPTER THREE

VOYAGE OF SURPRISE

For some reason my thoughts stayed with the beautiful memories of Singapore as I showered and dressed for the new day.

I remembered going alone to church every Sunday and reading the younger ones stories about Jesus at Sunday School. I recalled an exciting visit with my classmates from school to Long San Chee Temple. The teacher also told us it was known as Dragon Mountain Temple, which conjured up wonderful imaginings to a young child of a quite different cultural background. We were told it was dedicated to Kwan Yin, the Taoist Goddess of Mercy. We were all lined up in front of the altar with the image of Confucius, and a prayer was said asking on behalf of our parents for intelligence to be bestowed on us all, together with filial piety.

One memory I have is as bizarre as it is inexplicable, and concerned my very first day at school. Mum put me on a bus with a group of other children from the flats where we lived. Of course I was only seven years old, very shy and in a foreign country. To add to my ordeal it was a new school and I was travelling with complete strangers. All went well until the end of the day when, no matter how hard I tried, I couldn't find the children I had set out with in the morning. Eventually I saw a bus stop and a bus so I did the obvious thing, I got on it. The bus stopped and started, stopped and started and, finally stopped altogether - at the terminus. A man in uniform with a smiling face found me in tears hiding behind a seat and jabbered in a language I could not understand. Then the police arrived. I was questioned by an interpreter who I could only just understand and told him my name was Nicola Stevens. Various checks were made and several hours later an officer announced a family called Barker had lost a seven year old child who answered to the name Nicola. Soon the mystery was unravelled.

When I arrived home I began to chew the glass while drinking water. The blood ran down spreading rapidly and covering the front of my white school blouse. Mum was furious and at her wits end - I felt a gentle peace as the traumatic and frustrating emotions of the day drained slowly away with my blood. This proved to be the only major blip for me during an idyllic life experience, it also perhaps suggested all was still not well in my tiny world.

Sadly, all good things come to an end, and although Dad did complete an extension to his contract, four years almost to the day after we arrived we prepared to set sail back to England. Emmy cried and we all cried too. The little friends I had made and whose names I still remember came to say goodbye through a deep sadness. There was another sad aspect of that last week. I had a pet duck I called Webster, and he went missing the day before we were due to leave. On the final night in Singapore we had a goodbye dinner party which gave Mum and Dad an opportunity to say farewell to their friends. Years later I recalled the menu had been duck! Webster? I have never eaten one since.

* * * * * * * * * * *

The passenger cargo liner 'Chitral,' originally named 'Jadotville,' was a thirteen thousand ton vessel owned by P & O. She was first off-the-blocks in 1956, capable of seventeen knots, had a cargo capacity of eleven thousand, three hundred and ninety cubic metres and carried two hundred and twenty six passengers as well as two hundred and fourteen crew. One of the crew was a Chinese steward called Paul. In about half-an-hour he managed to destroy four years of mental and physical healing. Such was his charm, I do not have quite the same hate and loathing for him that I have for many of the others who shaped my life.

It was 1967 and the Chitral was about to make a voyage that would provide London with its first ever containerised cargo of Japanese salmon, it would also return our family to the UK for good.

I had been seven years of age on the outward plane journey and, although filled with awe in one respect, once the initial thrill of taking off was complete, I had been bored. On this journey however, I was going to celebrate my eleventh birthday and explored the ship from stem to stern as any excited child of that age would do. Mum and Dad rarely saw me. I would spend most of the day helping with the young children in the crèche, playing games and generally amusing them. I loved every second. Once while exploring I discovered a place where some dogs were being kennelled while in transit to Britain, I was horrified because they were starving. They were so thin you could count their ribs and I hatched a plan. At every meal time I discreetly collected as much food as I could without being seen and took it to the upper deck where the poor animals were suffering. I would not have been impressed had I known they were a valuable racing strain of greyhound on a special diet; by the time they reached Britain you could no longer count their ribs...!

As the Chitral approached Egypt, Mum, Dad and Felicity decided we would all go over land rather than pass through the Suez Canal in order to see the pyramids, Cairo and much more. I was indignant. I loved the ship, it was to be my birthday and the Captain had said I could have a special party. And of course I had my dogs to feed!

Exasperated, Mum had words in the appropriate quarters and it was arranged for me to remain on board alone overnight - my minder was to be a Chinese steward, his name was Paul.

The party was wonderful and I felt like a princess as I headed for my cabin at bedtime. Mum had threatened me with a fate worse than death if I did not behave impeccably, and with a final flourish of her index finger told me Paul was to be in total charge.

Once the door was closed behind me and I was in the privacy of my cabin, I danced around in my party dress to imaginary music, reliving the extravaganza put on especially for a birthday-girl by the Captain of the ship. Eventually, I undressed and put on my pyjama suit jacket, beginning to feel a little sleepy as the adrenalin slowed. I paused as I went to remove my knickers which was Mother's number one rule of the night. Rebelliously I yanked them back up and pulled on the trouser bottoms with a sense of satisfaction at being able to do my 'own thing'. I lay on my bunk separated from the humidity of the night only by a sheet and dozed fitfully, only occasionally becoming wide awake as some part of the moving ship interrupted sleep. Suddenly, the door made a noise as it slowly opened and I could just see Paul the steward through half an eye in the semi-darkened cabin. The door closed and I thought he had gone satisfied I was asleep. It was only then I realised he was standing in the shadows, an enormous and beautiful smile on his oriental features and without speaking he walked towards me. My eyes closed hoping he would not chastise me for being awake. Had he noticed my eyes had been open? Everything was still for a minute or maybe more and curiosity forced me to take a look. His head was about two feet from mine, still smiling his friendly smile - I smiled back.

Gently he pulled back the sheet and my heart sank; Mum must have told him I would break a rule and wear my knickers. He put a finger under the elastic waistband of my pyjama bottoms and pulled them down about an inch. I was lying on my side and he let go of the elastic gently and rolled me onto my back, simultaneously pulling my legs out straight in front of me.

Slowly, he knelt on the bunk by my side and I felt both his hands probe gently under my waist and gradually pulled down my pyjama trousers. The game was up, now I would be in trouble when Mum returned. Still, at least he did not shout in anger or tell me off and spoil my party night. His hands went back to my waist. This time I lifted up my bottom, there seemed no point in arguing and he slipped off my knickers very, very slowly. It crossed my mind he had done so because he thought he would wake me, but I dismissed it because my eyes were open and although preoccupied I knew he had noticed. He placed the two items of clothing on a chair in the corner and then returned to stand and look down at me. I squeezed my legs together tightly in slight embarrassment then became puzzled as he began to undo the buttons on my top. He opened both sides leaving me naked apart from the sleeves which still covered my arms. Gently he stroked the nipples on my undeveloped breasts with the cushions of his fingers, and I shivered visibly and thought of how Auntie Joan had loved me. The tickle was pleasant and I felt the whole of my body shudder as his fingers slid slowly to my belly button. Then gently in a circular caressing motion around my tummy and finally halt at the top of where my legs were still firmly held together. The fingers tried to probe between, but could not. Throughout, my eyes had not left his face, now he was looking at me again, still smiling the same beautiful smile. I thought of Billy Goat Gruff, of nights long ago and how he had loved me too, but how could this man love me? I had only known him briefly. His fingers probed the tightness again, I relaxed the pressure and opened my legs slightly. Hardly touching my flesh he stroked the area he could reach and with a dry mouth I savoured mysterious sensations - I opened my legs further.

It was then he moved to the bottom of the bunk and gradually parted my legs lifting them until they bent at the knees. Delicately his lips touched each of my nipples, his tongue probed my belly button then sank deeply between my legs. It was a slow, licking and sucking motion that, though noiseless, seemed to penetrate to my very soul - then he was gone, not a word spoken.

I was swept by a wave of confusion. Echoes of Braunton House with its love and ecstasy yet sinister shades of grey. Now the confusing encounter with my Chinese steward, spine-tingling, fabulous, yet an indefinable overtone of culpability. Nothing of my wonderous life in Singapore bore confrontation of an intimate nature. No part of my life with the Barkers contained any form of secrecy or acts that had to be hidden in the hours of daylight. I was beginning to realise right from wrong.

The following day I could barely face him but was made to comply by returning parents, who innocently considered I owed him a debt of gratitude. My naivety was such I would be racked with torment for months to come, thinking I was pregnant as a result of an ordeal of which they had no knowledge.

The creak of the davits became the frame of the hotel bed, the Chitral's engines the traffic outside the hotel window in the busy street, the glistening object in my hand the steel of a razor blade. It was with enormous effort I returned it to my case....unused.

CHAPTER FOUR

THE BALCONY

My blood father Arthur, murdered his second wife by pushing her off the balcony of his third floor flat when they were both drunk. He told me the story with an evil leer on his drunken face one night when in a killing mood, and took great pleasure in repeating it many times together with stories of other crimes he had got away with, often when I met him in pubs in front of other evil men. I was there only for free drink - the lengths to which I would go to satisfy my addiction knew no bounds. 'No evidence against me, I got away with killing the evil bitch!' He spat the words with saliva just missing me. Today I intended to visit the place where he had lived, she had died and he had raped me.

These seemingly innocent looking domestic premises held the most horrendous of memories for me. Despite this, the most keenly etched psychological scars which stood firm for the duration of my life even including the horror of later years, were simple school playground taunts made by other children.

'I read about your Dad in the papers again, he's in court more often than the magistrates! - Your Dad's in jail, my mummy told me! - Your Dad was so drunk in the park he couldn't stand up! - He tried to put his hand up my skirt!'

Poor Felicity was in the same school for a short time, one day I heard her explaining to friends we had different parents and I was only her foster sister. I didn't know why, but I felt humiliated.

Arthur had a lot of women when he was drunk, which he nearly always was, and as a consequence there were several offspring. I died in shame and confusion each time younger kids came up to me announcing they were my brother or sister.

Arthur was an evil man, drunk or sober, although he became a softie in his later years according to my eldest sister Sarah, who had befriended him in his old age. It was difficult for me to associate good in any way, shape or form to a so-called father who had abused me terribly, and strangled our cats and dogs with his bare hands.

Only a few weeks previously I had visited my brother Roy, with whom I was now reconciled after a fifteen year break. There was a picture of him as a little boy on the sideboard, smiling and handsome, I remarked how little he had changed, apart from losing his hair. 'It's not me it's our Dad,' he had said - I was aghast. How could such a lovely little boy turn into an evil monster? I suddenly realised I had spoken the words aloud. We had gone on to discuss the man with whom we shared a blood tie and I remember experiencing considerable surprise that his memories were somewhat different to mine. He had very few recollections of Arthur as a child, but as a young adult they drank together and got involved in fights with others and frequently with each other.

I gazed up at Dad's former flat, slightly unsure if it was the second or third floor. I recalled the night he told me of his wife's demise and the reason being that it was because of her insane nagging and drunkeness. He was holding a knife at my throat at the time threatening me with the same fate. The ordeal remains one of my worst.

I shuddered as I looked down at the concrete path which lay beneath the balcony and imagined the impact of flesh and bone on the rough solid surface. His word against nobody else's I thought to myself. I considered my rekindled religious beliefs and decided he would one day answer to the Almighty for his sins. It was for sure that all five of us would have only suffered more had the family not been split up.

The Barkers were very kind to me though they had some odd ways, but I was treated quite differently to Felicity. Nevertheless I am more than grateful for the good years they brought me, though extremely sad at the way it came to an end.

Felicity was eighteen. She had fallen in love with someone Mum and Dad did not approve of and the rows were unceasing. Finally, she packed her belongings and left home to join Adam, her new-found beau. I was devastated. I cried every night and was torn between the Barker's parental indignation, their obvious hurt and constant reminders to me that if I had anything to do with Felicity whatsoever behind their backs, I would be guilty of the ultimate betrayal.

Felicity meanwhile, wanted me more than ever before. She lay in wait for me on my way to school and told me how important I was to her which was everything I had ever yearned for. 'There are a few things I need. Take this list, bring them to me here tomorrow at the same time,' she had said with an arm around my shoulders holding me tightly.

The next day Mum caught me leaving the house and asked if I was secretly meeting their wicked daughter. I could not lie, said yes and was told for my pains that I was even worse than Felicity. Life was never the same again at the Barkers. Felicity was eventually forgiven and welcomed back into the fold - life continued to be odd for me despite their concerted efforts to provide a good home. They had strange ideas and inexplicable rules. I could only wash my hair once a week. This was awful for me as I had extremely greasy hair, and I had to manage with just one pack of sanitary towels for the duration no matter how severe my condition. Worst of all was clothes shopping. As a foster child this fact was announced at the checkout to explain why payment was made in part cash and vouchers supplied by what was then called the 'welfare department.' I stood often, dying a death within, looking around me convinced everyone was looking at my inadequacy. No doubt there were very good reasons for their behaviour, but as a child I could not understand and still cannot to this day. Of one thing I am quite certain, they were good people who only meant well, and their motives would have been out of misguided, old-fashioned upbringings of their own, rather than malice aforethought. To compound my mental instability I had endured a terrible experience a year after our return from Singapore.

I was twelve at the time and a year into my new school and perversely a safe English way of life after a four year absence. One day I was walking from my school at the end of lessons when I approached a building being refurbished with canvas covered scaffolding adjacent to the pavement. A man in working clothes called out to me and asked if I could help him free a trapped fellow worker. He looked panic stricken and I followed him as quickly as I could in order to keep up because he was running.

I followed him through a doorway and up a flight of stairs and at the top, I realised for the final time that Auntie Joan, Billy Gruff and Paul the Chitral steward, definitely did not love me. Another man sat in the corner on an old mattress swigging from a bottle, he took one look at me and staggered to his feet. The first man pushed me down onto the mattress. I was terrified and began to cry and shouted at the top of my voice. Then I felt a stunning blow at the base of my skull.

I do not know how long I was unconscious, but it could only have been seconds because I awoke to hear them discussing my fate.

'Did anyone see you bring her in?' It was the man with the bottle who had spoken and he slurred his words making it difficult for me to follow what he said. 'No-one, I'm certain,' the original man was undoing his belt and pulling down his zip. I curled up pulling my knees up under my chin. I was wearing a skirt bought by my mother during one of our embarrassing shopping expeditions and it was six inches below the knee. The fashion at the time was more like six inches above the knee and as a consequence, once out of sight of home, I rolled the waistband over and over until the length was in vogue. The other man, who had now put down his bottle, was holding an iron bar instead and looking at me threateningly snarled, 'one more sound out of you and I'll crush your head like a walnut.'

I knew what a penis was. Next to my school was another place of education for backward boys and girls and one day during a lunchtime walk, a friend and I saw six or seven of them, trousers down around their ankles gripping their enormous 'things' and shaking them backwards and forwards. We were asked if we wanted to touch and hold and play. Curious, intrigued and fascinated we did. They were all hard, very hard though different lengths and thicknesses and a white creamy liquid shot out of the first one I touched almost at once. The second took longer and the third showed

no sign at all so I gave up bored. I remembered
Billy Gruff and recalled the white cream, there was
more to this than I could understand. I concluded
there must be, because it was all in secret and no-
one seemed to want to speak about it; I wondered
if I was doing wrong?

The first man was now removing his underpants and he came towards me and ordered me to
lie out flat on my back, he held his penis in his
hand shaking it roughly back and forth like the
boys in the school next door had done. I refused to
move. The second man lifted the iron bar menac-
ingly and I lay back in terror. He knelt down beside
me putting the iron bar down by my head and said
in almost a whisper 'Have you ever been fucked?'
Thoughts of past experiences told me I might have
been, but I shook my head. 'Stand up!' He thundered. Shakily I rose to my feet. He rose too,
removed my blazer and began to undo the buttons
on my school blouse. He put his hand inside and
pinched the nipples on my newly forming breasts
and kneaded them while I squealed in pain, then
he pulled out the blouse from where it was tucked
into my school uniform skirt - then undid the skirt
itself. I felt it down around my ankles and his fingers gouging roughly inside my knickers. He
forced what seemed like half his hand up deep
inside me and I suddenly became aware of the second man trying to do the same while they argued
loudly over who was going first. I screamed in
agony!

Barely conscious, I was vaguely aware of the

hysterical type of laughter I associate with drunkeness in my adult life as they played their evil game. Then abruptly the arrival of a third man. Much louder even angrier shouting and scuffling and blows being dealt, screams of pain, the sounds of running footsteps, then a calm kindly voice asking if I was O.K. A man who vaguely reminded me of a builder I saw regularly on a television soap opera was gently tapping my cheeks and I came to with a start. 'O.K, O.K don't be frightened. I heard you screaming, it's all right now. Get dressed and I'll take you to the police station.'

I got dressed. Thanked him in sobbing tones but said no to the police, the last time I went to a police station in Singapore I was there for hours. He tried to persuade me, said they were wicked men. I was adamant, Mum would be angry and when she was angry with me she often said I would be sent back to the children's home. Fear possessed its own territory in my mind. Auntie Joan had an agenda of her own, I knew not why specifically, but memories of love had shifted to questions inspiring innuendo and insinuations of insider dealing of a non-financial nature. No matter what, I no longer wanted to go back to the home. For the rest of my life I would cross over the road or change direction rather than go near scaffolding or a building site. I knew then, for the remainder of my days, I would do a great deal of suffering secretly and in silence.

I looked back at the balcony from which my father had proudly admitted to having committed his terrible crime, decided that death would have been instantaneous, and walked slowly back to the town centre.

CHAPTER FIVE

GENTLE JESUS

The reality was my home town held a mixture of memories that at best I would describe as miserable, and at worst hideous. The year that followed my ordeal was probably the most focused of my life, I came second in my class and top in Religious Instruction. I immersed myself in Christianity because I suddenly suspected that sex was sex, love was God only knows what, and for reasons I could now associate only with sin, I had been extremely wicked.

During the month that followed my ordeal I had terrible nightmares and was undoubtedly in a state of dementia. Quite suddenly, during a quiet moment with my R.I. teacher, Miss Lewis, I gleaned from her that God loved little children, and she taught me the prayer that ended.... 'Suffer me to come to thee'. I asked her if God would forgive whatever terrible things I might have done. She said. 'My dear little one, how could you possibly have done anything unforgivable?' I was still not altogether sure how much of the sin was mine, how much belonged to other people, or if it was simply my just desserts. Nevertheless, I felt better and the rest of the year transpired to be my best ever academically. It was disturbed by only one event which, from beginning to end, lasted no more than fifteen seconds.

I had joined a new pupil who had arrived from Australia, for a walk around the tennis courts one lunch time. Her name was Jane Cartwright and quite suddenly, for no reason I can explain despite pondering it a thousand times, she threw her arms around my neck and kissed me passionately on the lips. It was the most beautiful kiss of my entire life.

I had already received excellent end of term examination results and was on a natural high. I was almost fourteen years of age now and the experience revived sensations of long ago, although a more mature version. Two weeks later Jane invited me to a party. 'Most of them will be older than us, so there will be lots of fun.' Jane sounded grown-up. I felt enormously privileged and an indescribable excitement.

Inexplicably, the peace I found from my R.I teacher Miss Lewis and the wonders of reading the scriptures and teaching the young ones at Sunday School, disappeared as if they had never existed. I told my Mum and Dad a pack of lies, and upon meeting Jane in the late afternoon at her house, borrowed some extremely fashionable and very short clothes. I remember arriving at the party. I was recommended a 'special' for my first drink, and the older boys around me like flies telling me how beautiful I was provided a high comparable to the drink, which was my very first ever experience with alcohol. My head was swimming and the euphoria and confidence in the form of adrenalin surging through my veins was outstanding. I fought hands attempting to grope my breasts and several bolder characters (or drunker) pulling up my skirt. I was overawed by the attention and the variation of pleas and chat-up lines attempting to win my favours. It gave me an enormous feeling of power over men that I have heard other women describe thousands of times since. I overheard another girl describe me as a slut - I asked what it meant, now I knew love was wrong. I managed to stay intact and unattached and even arrived home in my own clothes at the agreed time.

There was a downside however which would dominate the rest of my life. The alcoholic high.

It had gone with the dawn and was replaced by the most awful remorse and depression imaginable. A thousand thoughts crowded my mind. Questions covering a lifetimes mysteries and pleasures bursting from lips that would never speak. Alcohol-induced dementia became the norm. The Barkers were at their wits end and months of my life sped by leaving no recollections only confrontations. I had no explanations for my behaviour - I know now I was breaking down mentally. I had stopped requesting permission to stay out late at night, walked away from reprimands and demanded a regime on my terms. I would walk for miles and miles, strike up conversations with people I did not know and became obsessed with the sins I had committed in the name of love. Never an hour in any day passed without me re-living the experiences that I now recognise as sex-ual, lustful and evil. One day I sat alone on a bench in a local park that was so large you could lose yourself - I was already a lost soul and at a complete loss on how to quantify the difference between good and bad. Alcohol had become a reg-ular and highly desirable addition to my life. On the occasions I felt depressed I took an extra swig from wherever it was most easily available. This day it came from a man who joined me on my bench.

I had long since discovered from girl-chat that full sex was not one of my experiences after all, and my apparent virginity was beginning to be a nuisance. I was running out of ideas to describe my latest conquest when the girls gathered to tell of their most recent adventures, and as it became more and more of a necessity not to be a virgin in order to attain womanhood, I felt an urgency to get it over with.

'Why are you crying?' The voice belonged to the man, who was about the same age as my fos-ter father and I wiped away the tears quickly. He was such a nice man. He spoke to me gently and I told him all my problems, the words just tumbled out. He explained the answers to everything in a manner which was so simple to understand I was amazed I had not worked it out for myself. All that was wrong, at home and throughout, was because I was changing from child to woman. One small matter, and one matter only, had to be completed, I had to have full sexual intercourse as soon as possible to make the transition complete. In a manner which, through his skills became far too beautiful to destroy with further conversation, he led me behind a small group of bushes and undressed me. The act itself was forgettable and a means to an end as far as I as concerned. From beginning to end it lasted five minutes and as he climbed to his feet I almost laughed at his pot belly hanging earthwards. The switch from being mesmerized by his words and kindness, to amusement even hilarity as he nearly fell over trying to struggle back into his old fashioned underpants, was momentary. Unexpectedly my mind posed the question, was he the definitive 'dirty old man' I had heard so much about? I observed, even as he thanked me for my favours, this had not been for my benefit and pondered confusingly if I had provoked, even corrupted, yet another human being with my evil attractions. Or was it vice versa? The brief humour was gone, I returned to the Barkers, but only after swigging a can of cider an off-licence proprietor sold to a fourteen and a half year childwoman in school uniform.

* * * * * * * * *

The following year August summer holidays arrived and I was bored. My latest friend was

53

Sheila Ward, she was having a party and I was first to be invited. I knew it would cause another row so I decided against telling my parents as it was to be an all night affair. I could not go through another inquisition, I was sick and tired of being told what to do. Who did they think they were anyway? They were not my real parents and were always threatening to send me back to the children's home if I did not behave.

Saturday came, the sun was shining and I was in the perfect frame of mind for a great time and to get drunk! I now had a permanent relationship with alcohol, gained at several venues particularly the local rugby club on the occasions I managed to get away from home. I had to travel ten miles to reach Sheila's house and I had very little money so I guessed it was to be a hitchhiking exercise. With hindsight, I'm not sure if I was getting hardened or just recklessly impervious to danger, because I saw it as good for a laugh. I think it was the thrill of not knowing what might happen. I had begun to like danger even though my heart used to beat so fast and furiously I thought it would burst. My quality of life was diminishing, the prospect of rape or murder posed little threat.

I had to wear my normal clothes when I left the house so as not to arouse suspicion. I put my evening attire together with forbidden make-up, in a separate bag and left the moment my parents departed for the weekly shop. Poignantly, I recall looking back at the house as I left and thinking I no longer viewed them as a mum and dad. They were authority, the establishment.

I walked to the main road which was sufficiently far away so as not to be spotted by tell-tale neighbours, and began thumbing traffic as it thundered by. The lift did not happen straight away and I regretted not being able to show a leg which I knew would secure a ride. Someone might recognise me, I couldn't have it all ways, I had to make good my escape. I had walked for about half an hour when a car stopped. He was an older man with a nice smile and patted the seat beside him, I got in and secured the safety belt - I was on my way.

It was less than thirty minutes drive and the man had little to say. Usual questions. How old? Where are you going? Do you have a boyfriend? Not exactly one of my most exciting journeys. Once he had dropped me off I had to ask directions because I was unfamiliar with the area.

I arrived early and there was little happening except for the music which was very loud. There were only about a dozen other early arrivals and no-one I knew other than Sheila. She originated from Yorkshire and had a distinct accent, was quite short, stocky build and wore her hair short, in fact she was very much a tomboy. On the other hand I had very long brown hair, was medium build and did everything I could to look feminine. I had recently become conscious of my weight as a result of a friend of my mother's describing me as chubby. I had started to watch my diet very closely and it was beginning to affect my life because I really loved my food. It had somehow left a dark cloud.

I secured a drink via a young guy who also looked lost. He seemed friendly enough to pass the time with, but not my type. I preferred my men older, not boys who were shy, had little to say and even less money. People began to arrive and lots of laughter ensued as they proceeded to drink to excess, I was happy to join in. It did not take much alcohol to loosen my tongue and get chatty with anyone who would listen, I had no idea why, but I always seemed to start telling my entire life story to people I had only just met. They always listened, but when sober the following day I realised it must have given an extremely strange impression.

After a couple of hours things really began to liven up. Everyone was dancing and I loved to dance. It made me feel free in a liberated sort of way, just to be able to let my body gyrate without restriction. I also felt a great power over men when I moved. I knew they were watching me and I had begun to crave their attention. I was beginning to realise the only man who had ever treated me without ulterior sexual motives was my foster father, all the rest had used and abused me, so why I craved male attention was unclear.

Men were now dancing closely to me on all sides and the more attention I received, the more inspired I became to dance sexually. Before I knew it I had the floor to myself and I put on a display that was rapidly becoming a well rehearsed routine. My head, arms, legs, everything pulsated. I was oblivious to everyone and everything except the music: 'Maggie May,' 'Stairway To Heaven,' haunting music and I lay on the carpet retreating into a private, personal and wondrous world. I was dreaming. Someone was stroking my face, arms, breasts, stomach, thighs and then the most intimate of places. It felt wonderful, unlike anything I had ever encountered. Every part of my body was being touched at the same time. I opened my eyes to discover many faces admiring me. I closed them again for fear they would disappear, I wanted the sensations to continue forever, and if I was dreaming, I did not want to wake up. It was as if I was asleep, then awake, asleep, awake, conscious, unconscious, I had lost touch with reality. Different voices, different faces, different music, sheer heaven.

I opened my eyes - daybreak. I looked around the room. Naked bodies everywhere just lying where they had dropped. My head, and other parts throbbed and nausea swept over me as I tried to move. I was parched and felt pain I now know to be dehydration, I searched for the kitchen and downed at least two pints of water. Sheila appeared from upstairs clucking about how wonderful the party had been - all I wanted to do was die. I had incomplete memories, I was confused, I wanted to get away. In my dreams I had bodies crawling all over me, kissing me, touching me. At the time it was great! Oh! My God, what had I done?

I gathered my clothes together and went to

57

the bathroom. I splashed cold water over my face to try to make sense of it all, I should not have drunk so much, why oh why did I always do that? Always I had to get plastered... I dragged on my clothes and ran, I had to get away, no time for goodbyes, plenty for regrets.

Vaguely I recall the sun shining, a lovely warm morning and I wished someone else had my head. Slowly I walked along the road and decided to do so all the way home. I was most definitely not looking forward to facing my parents and the usual barrage of questions. The longer the delay the better.

I am not sure how long it took for me to walk home, I was not even aware of the time of day. They were there, in the front garden, trowels in hand the epitome of suburban respectability - Mum tried to talk to me, Dad looked bewildered. I went down the driveway and in through the back door straight to my room and hastily locked the door. I threw myself onto my bed and cried myself into a nightmarish sleep.

* * * * * * * * * * *

The more I thought of my decision to return to my home town, the more I was beginning to regret it. The idea had been to lay the ghosts living on in my subconscious that constantly plunged me in and out of depression. The reality of my journey was developing into what was seeming to be a re-run of my entire life. It had been bad enough the first time around, a second glance was proving just as painful and effectively revealing additional horrors hitherto missed or lost in the passage of time. I considered the option of cutting short my stay and returning from whence I came. I had almost returned home after the first day, only Hayley made me stay. She had no way of knowing of course, but her appearance had planted a seed and I was unable to prevent it growing.

I could still revive in my memory the sensations and feelings of confusions experienced as a schoolgirl when confronted by Arthur's offspring. Now they ran deeper, this confusion was mine, Hayley was closer to home. I decided to take my car out of the hotel garage and reconnoitre places presently living only in the annals of my mind. I wondered what Hayley would have thought of my top of the range luxury two-seater sports roadster, at least twenty thousand pounds sterling more expensive than the one which had attracted her to the new boyfriend. It was a stupid analogy, I was not in a competition with a young man for her affections, this was not the inspiration for my thoughts. My mind had always moved in an odd way, my real observation was centred on how I would have valued my car when I was Hayley's age. I knew the answer of course - it would have blown my mind.

Surprisingly, I spent an enjoyable day. Touring old haunts with myriads of memories, some good, mainly bad and then shopping, parking, shopping, parking and visiting the homes of old school pals or rather their mothers, and occasionally finding both parents still alive though now in mid-seventies. I was amazed how many still lived in the homes where they had brought up my school pals, I had a wonderful time swapping memories and had a book full of new addresses for old friends who needless to say had married and moved on.

I had one last call to make before returning to the hotel for dinner. I had to go to 23, Wood Street. It was difficult to locate and eventually I discovered it to be impossible, the street had completely disappeared and in its place, was an enormous Sainsbury's. I stood as near to the place where I first met insanity as my sense of direction and allowances for modern architecture would allow. I recalled the pain, confusion and the terrible phantasm. Chimera type, surreal and terrifying repetition of madness and illusions when my psyche switched alarmingly between this and perfect peace. I had been fifteen and seven months and it was the aftermath of my party of infamy. The memory was as vivid today as it was at the time...

One cloudy, dull, unforgettable morning I was crawling out of bed when an overwhelmingly sinister feeling came over me. I rushed to the bathroom and was violently sick. It suddenly dawned on me how my so-called party-night of wonderment through drunkeness, had truly climaxed - I was pregnant! It had to be. Missed periods, weight gain and now sickness and disorientation.

Thoughts of horror and terror alternately filled my head. How was I going to tell my parents?

What should I do? Where could I go? I had become a loner and had few options. My whole world was insular as a result of the hate I bore for myself; I had only ever brought evil into the lives of others! So I stood alone.

I recall it being a Saturday with a heavy frost. I had no set destination as I walked slowly into town, only a few possessions, precious photographs, a change of underwear. I found myself in the main city centre and sat down next to a group of hippie type characters on a wooden bench.

'You look pissed off.'

The voice belonged to a contented looking man in his early thirties, denim clad and beads, leather bracelets and rings in profusion.

'I'm bloody pregnant!' My voice was so loud I startled myself. A big smile spread over his friendly face. 'It's not the end of the world you know,' he said. 'Huh! It might not be for you,' I countered and we glared at one another.

His voice, deep baritone, had a calming effect and he asked me to tell him all about it. I didn't take much prompting I needed someone to listen to my ramblings. Encouraged by the arrival of several other male and female hippies and a few swigs from one of their lager cans, I proceeded to tell my life story.

'You can come and stay with us, we'll look after you for as long as it takes.' This was a new voice belonging to a woman in her middle thirties who had hitherto been listening to my story with deep concentration.

I was elated, and after a few more swigs we all trooped off together. I experienced a rare feeling of kinship as we marched, arm-in-arm, to 23 Wood Street.

CHAPTER SIX

THE MYSTERY OF THE DOOR TO AN INNER WORLD

We arrived, I was given a small but homely, ever so bohemian room of my own, a cotton nightie and two tablets I was told would help in my condition. Two of my new friends sat by the bed and I rambled, they listened and we smoked a large hand rolled cigarette by passing it from one to the other. The tablets had an immediate effect. I felt as good as I did when I had drunk a can of extra strong lager and the 'smoke' was something else. I floated in a wonderland of love and euphoria. The warmth radiating from my two immediate companions and numerous subsequent visiting brothers and sisters as they liked to be called, made the atmosphere electric. Just when I thought I was beginning to lose the buoyancy of my new found ecstatic elation, one of the sisters would bring my medication, and more often than not, a puff or two from one of those wonderful handmade cigarettes.

I floated a lot, but enjoyed only limited exercise in a weed-filled garden at the rear of the property. There were however moments of lucidity when I was able to consider what had become of me. I was privy albeit hazily, to a great deal of conversation between my new brothers and sisters, hearing phrases like drug addiction, alcoholism and a dozen other slang expressions too numerous to mention cropping up time and time again. I asked one of the girls what an alcoholic was. The only time I had actually heard it applied was at school when another girl once told me my real dad was an alcoholic. The hippie sister looked at me steadily for several seconds and then said almost dismissively, 'Hell! We're all bloody alcoholics.'

Hours, days, nights, weeks, passed in arcane, enigmatic yet inconsequential periods of incantation. An overwhelming and endless succession of the most beautiful love affairs passed through my psyche, with loving and caring men and women like Billy Gruff and Auntie Joan. Whether real, hallucination, wishful thinking or non compos mentis bordering total insanity, I knew not. There were also appalling encounters, intermittent and fewer in number punctuating the pleasures. Abuse, both physical and sexual were perpetrated by those who had first succored and adored. It was a price I was prepared to pay for the wonders I found when the door was opened to my magical and wonderous inner world. Occasionally, but only very occasionally, I experienced slight anxiety as the door to this spectacular place began to close. I need not have worried - my medication arrived, the pills, the big hand-rolled cigarettes and cans of cider and lager in abundance.

One day or night the inevitable happened, for nothing lasts forever. The door to the Inner World opened and in the place of pleasure I found hell.

Sleep and fitful bed-rest was my normal existence punctuated with my journeys through paradise. As the house began to settle on this night, at a period in time interminable to my disorientated mind, abruptly I perceived an atmospherical change. There was an ambience of stillness undisturbed by even the slightest creak of staircase or window casement. In a sudden explosion of burning pain and distorted sound, the monstrous apparition of the Devil in a vile spectre of evil, lunged itself at me and stabbed me in the stomach. The pain was indescribable. I writhed and screamed as the blade from Hades was torn from its deep wound and an unexpected realization dawned that I was no longer alone. Two of the devil's demonic helpers pulled my legs apart until I thought I would split down the middle. The blade was plunged deeply between my legs and blood and water spurted in all directions. A distant cry, or perhaps not. A babble of excited conversation. A voice of the human kind urging me to swallow tablets. Blankets were pulled up around me. I was shown a doll covered in blood and a white foam like substance. 'It's dead.' The voice was solemn and unforgiving. Not a doll - a new born child! I reached out to hold it - to this day I cannot bear the sight of death, even the smallest spider or fly,

a mouse or rabbit would instantly become someone's baby.

It was a little girl born prematurely. I called
her Hayley in my subconscious and would mourn
her for the remainder of my life.

CHAPTER SEVEN

HEARTBREAK HOTEL

That night I dined alone. Cornelius and his fellow professionals had moved on to pastures new and there were fewer residents in the hotel, for the time being anyway.

I was actually quite pleased. It gave me an opportunity to relax in relative peace and quiet, something I needed after the traumas of the day. I had been quite calculated and determined in my efforts to fix the exact position of number 23, Wood Street. I recalled an old nineteenth century horse trough twenty yards from where the front door had once been. It was still there, now protected by English Heritage and the room in which I had spent so much time in my other life, was a further ten yards back. I worked out the distance with footsteps and smiled a macabre smile - the place where I had met Satan now housed pork pies.

I had a simple scampi and french fries from the menu and had almost finished eating when I saw Angie Dixon. My blood ran cold. Probably the closest I ever came to a violent death was when I was under her spell. Discreetly I signed my bill the moment I completed my meal, and slipped out of the restaurant without her noticing me. Despite the horrors of my involvement with her, fear was not the motive, I was actually keen to meet up with her again but now was just not the time.

It had taken much soul searching over several years to persuade myself to embark upon my journey of remembrance, and the whole exercise had been planned like a military operation. I returned to my room and lay on the bed propped up with two large pillows and a good book.

I had only read a couple of pages when I realised my mind was wandering back to the mysteries of the door to my inner world. It was no longer a mystery of course - it had been solved long ago by masters of their trade. Had it not been so I could not have made this trip, nevertheless it was always going to be an ordeal. I'd had more than enough time to reflect upon the delicate balance and terrifying fragility of the human mind. Disturbingly, there was frequently for me, a perceptible intermediary, usually malevolent, between a rational mentality and my brush with insanity. I pondered on the day I had left the hippies and, as usual, felt a surge of anger due to elements of which I was now mindful. I recalled the medication and those wonderful cigarettes ceasing to be a part of each day. No longer did I get my cans of amber nectar, only the tablets remained. Within a very short time I shook, sweated and suffered an anxiety and remorse beyond conventional human discernment. It was not long before a previously friendly face said I would have to go - they needed my room for someone in greater need. I collected a few possessions together slowly, perhaps in the vain hope they would change their minds. They did not, and I walked aimlessly away in a state of confusion. I became aware of a metal object I was turning over and over in my pocket and pulled it out to see what it was. My front door key to the Barker's house stared back up at me and I headed for home. With hindsight I find it extremely difficult to imagine how they must have felt. Hearing a key in the lock, looking up in surprise, probably even sheer amazement as their wayward foster daughter wandered in two months late for lunch. Refusing to answer questions appertaining to, 'Where? Why? How?' No explanation whatsoever, just a stunned and sullen silence. Locked in her room for ten days only slinking out at night, rejecting all efforts to talk to the visiting GP.

Withdrawal from the drugs began almost immediately upon my return home. The physical aspect was so violent on the third day, my body convulsed in a manner I have difficulty in describing. I only know I had lost control of my faculties. Every muscle vibrated involuntarily and my teeth seemed to be rattling in my head, no matter how hard I tried I could not lie still. I felt a pain which grew in severity somewhere around the heart and I was convinced I was about to die. If this were not enough to contend with, I had a dry mouth that was so severe it was chapped inside, I was vomiting constantly and on occasions of unconsciousness, fought with demons and frequently an apparition I defined as the Devil himself. As best I can recall, the worst of what I now know to be withdrawal from drugs, components of which I can only speculate upon, lasted five or six days. At its conclusion I was totally exhausted and could not stir, movement came at a snail's pace and was excruciatingly painful due to acute cramp emanating from lack of exercise.

'Shit!' I exclaimed aloud looking back in time from the safety of my hotel room. 'Was I ill!!'

I rang through to the reception and asked for room service. 'Can I assist madam?' The perfectly normal voice sounded odd at that moment because much of my head was back in the past, or in what I perceived as my 'other incarnation.' I winced as I reflected on the internal damage created by lack of simple healthcare, and the pain I suffered over subsequent years as a result. Disease and operations would follow and I would never successfully bear a child again. 'Would you be so kind as to send a pot of coffee up to room eight?' I sounded normal enough, but then of course I was reliving in flashbacks. No matter how hard I tried, always assuming I was that way inclined, I could never satisfactorily re-enter the mind of that fifteen year old who believed absolutely she was being punished by God, and who knelt in tears hour after hour incessantly reciting lines from her Bible. Perhaps it was just as well.

Another week passed. I was alive physically - mentally I functioned only within my own insanity. Talking to imaginary people, living make-believe lives, frequently alongside one another. Always jumbled, never free of hate, loathing and utter revulsion for myself and the evil I spread; Bible in hand, I vowed to stay away from decent people so as not to contaminate them. One image remains a pitiful memory. Clutching God's book a movement caught my attention through my bedroom window - a young girl I knew was walking by in a pretty summer dress innocently holding hands with her boyfriend smiling happily. Why could this not be me? I cried myself to sleep.

The next day was a Monday. I got up, put on my school uniform, joined a shell-shocked family for breakfast and went to school. I'd always had a particular friend I sat next to in class. When I entered the classroom she was sitting alone, I gave her only a cursory glance and took a desk by myself. At lessons I listened intently and took my exams within months of my return and obtained satisfactory results. At the end of each day I hurried home, ate tea in silence, then went to my room and cried for my baby. One day, my sixteenth birthday, I walked to a local cemetery and scanned the area for a small stone that bore no name. I found one, it said simply 'Gone to Jesus'. I wrote above it a single word with an art brush from a small tin of black model paint taken from school. 'Hayley', my favourite name, taken from she who had brought me pleasure in a film called

'Whistle Down The Wind'. The following day I returned with a small bouquet of flowers purchased with savings from a meagre allowance given by my parents. I placed them gently below the stone and said a prayer aloud.

As my thoughts returned to the present and the luxury of my hotel room, I felt a deep sadness for this little soul who lived only in my past. Then the thoughts turned to anger. I had returned to 23, Wood Street one final time some months after the experience in search of I know not what. The house was empty with a FOR SALE sign on show. The next door neighbour told me they had only rented and were now living in a nice new house at the other side of town adding; 'How they could have possibly afforded it, I do not know.' She had said it was a mystery. It was beginning to become less of one to me, as a terrible suspicion crossed my mind.

CHAPTER EIGHT

IT COULD HAVE BEEN ME

At the hotel the following morning I awoke to an early call, a tray of coffee and the morning paper. The headline screamed out

WOMAN CAUGHT ON HOSPITAL VIDEO STEALING BABY

The story went on to describe the hell suffered by the family, criticism of the hospital maternity unit security procedures and the evil of the perpetrator. My mouth was dry and I trembled slightly as I considered how it could have been me.

I had walked into the maternity unit at my local hospital shortly after losing my child and stood staring at the babies. No-one asked any questions, I even cradled one despite it being hooked up with tubes, and whispered 'I love you Hayley' - the infant just slept on, oblivious of the experience. I never went again because the next day the local paper contained an advertisement for a mother's help.

'Patricia is four weeks old on Monday and Michael is twenty one months.' Mother and I sat opposite my prospective employer in a sumptuous bungalow on the edge of town, and nodded and shook our heads in all the right places. It was Mrs. Zipoli who had spoken the words. Mr. Zipoli sat next to her, smiling and gesticulating as all Italians seem to do, adding an air of friendliness to the proceedings. Eleanor and Gianni, as they would become, were a stark contrast to one another. He was handsome and full of fun though a hard worker. She was English, noticeably younger than he, seemingly void of personality and not surprisingly delighted when I accepted the position at the prospect of never having to work in the home again, if the terms of employment were anything to go by.

My week began when the baby awoke at six a.m. on Tuesday mornings and stretched without a break bar five hours sleep nightly, for six days - Monday, all day and night were mine. My official title was mother's help, unofficially I was a skivvy on call twenty four hours a day. However, I ceased to think of hours from the moment I met baby Patricia and her brother Michael. My world of make-believe took only a slight change of direction, the children were living proof of my claims to motherhood and wedded bliss. Although days out were limited by the overwhelming workload, I did manage them from time-to-time. When I did, I would deliberately involve myself in conversations with people I met on bus trips away from home and tell a grand tale. The elder child was a difficult birth but my husband, a restaurateur, had paid for a private hospital place and likewise the younger etc. etc. etc. However, such a day out was far from a suitable description of a normal day. One of these would be quite different and I've wondered a thousand times since, how I managed. Shortly after six a.m. I bathed and dressed the baby who was already awake, I did likewise for Michael and took morning tea to the Zipolis together with the morning papers. The kitchen was a sight once seen you would never forget. Incredibly, they would spend all day at work from ten a.m. in the morning, rarely coming home during the day although Gianni sometimes did, arrive home at midnight and frequently later, then cook themselves a meal. Debris resembling a battlefield greeted me daily, it never crossed my mind to do anything other than clear it up, so I did. By five to ten they were gone for the day and I proceeded to do everything necessary to care for and occupy, two infants and the not to be underestimated job of housework. One consolation reigned supreme - I was their mother.

The bungalow was beautiful even luxurious, yet amazingly there was no washing machine. I smiled ruefully at the memory as I gazed through my hotel window, of six plastic buckets in the kitchen strategically placed in line, to accommodate all necessary separation for the forthcoming weekly wash. And I did the lot with my bare hands until they were raw. My wages were less than a fifth of the national average wage paid for a forty hour week - my hours, virtually incalculable.

Days ran into weeks ran into months. My tortured mind recalls very little, though some memories do exist. I can never forget waking, screaming from the horror of endless nightmares. Frequently Eleanor would shake me into wakefulness in the dead of night, then leave me sobbing into my pillow when I longed for a hug or simple word of comfort. The child in me yearned for a mother's love, although I am not sure I identified it as such at the time, I just felt an utter alienation bereft of bond or link to my fellow mortals. For some of this I had only myself to blame. I had deliberately and calculatedly severed all connections with the Barkers. I did not return their phone calls and ripped up letters without reading them. It was vital for me to have no-one in my world who could remind me I was not mother to the children.

Through all this I had one connection to the human race, albeit flimsy and as childlike as my own capricious mental condition, her name was Samantha and she was eight. The first time I saw her was during a walk in the park with Patricia and Michael. She was with two kids of around her own age and spotting my charges playing with a ball, she skipped up to me and asked if mine could come and play with them. I told her to fuck off. She replied by commenting how much Patricia was like me, I beamed and decided she was a delightful child, the way to my heart was through my mind.

76

I saw her pretty much, once a week. Her fantasy was that she would come and live with me when she left school and look after the children. I let her dream on, she was my only link with the real outside world and such was my mental state life otherwise passed by without me.

One hundred and eighteen people died in Heathrow Airport's worst ever crash without me knowing and the American ground combat units left Vietnam. A band of Black September Arab guerrillas broke into the Israeli building in the Munich Olympic Village and massacred a wrestling coach and ten members of the team, all without me. I washed dirty clothes by hand for the entire household without the slightest inkling of Watergate rumblings and had absolutely no idea that Picasso had died. I must have been the only tennis fanatic in the world who did not know of the players' boycott of the Wimbledon Tournament over the suspension of a Yugoslav player. And despite an almost immaculate recollection of tennis records, studied throughout my life, I cannot recall a single item of interest from the time about eventual winner Jan Kodes of Czechoslovakia. My seventeenth birthday came and went unnoticed.

One thing does stand out however, like a beacon in a storm-lashed sea. We all sat as a family and watched every second of Princess Anne's wedding to Captain Mark Phillips on television. Ironically, as things turned out, I viewed the whole celebration with a great deal of cynicism. On reflection I wonder if it had some sort of effect upon me because one morning, just before Christmas, I was immersed in my mummy and children fantasy when I suddenly felt very silly. Almost immediately my imaginings switched to one of fear as a moment of lucidity allowed me a glimpse into my insanity. Was I being allowed a last glance at life as it really was by my Maker before I completely passed into oblivion? I picked up the telephone, dialled the restaurant and announced to an extremely startled Eleanor that I was going to leave their employ. 'What on earth has happened?' she asked incredulously. 'Nothing, I've just got to go,' was all I said and put down the receiver.

Eleanor and Gianni accepted the inevitable, although I suspect Eleanor found it easier to face up to because of a problem emerging for her as the children got older - they were calling me Mummy... of course!

The parting was amicable although both children screamed for me to stay, tears cascading down their little cheeks. Several weeks later I was working on a till in Marks and Spencers and Eleanor was in the queue with both the children. Neither child recognized me, which puts infants and their resilience firmly in perspective and Eleanor's charming if not smug smile fixed in my brain forever.

CHAPTER NINE

NEIL AND PRAY

Please dear God - help Neil to love me. Night after night I asked this first and foremost in my prayers.

I had first seen him as a twelve year old while on a weekend course from school with the Red Cross. He was three years older than me, as handsome as a film star and completely out of reach. On this day he was standing at my till paying for chicken breasts and oven chips and I was all fingers and thumbs. Had a supervisor not intervened I would have probably put the till permanently out of commission and suffered apoplexy....

Returning to the present and the peace and quiet of my hotel room, I became aware of the morning coffee tray still by my side as I reclined in bed. The coffee pot was stone-cold, my muscles stiff and I caught my breath in pain as I looked sideways at the clock which told me it was nearly lunchtime. Not for the first time on this trip I considered the folly of putting myself through such an ordeal for no reason I could think of, other than for Justin and the dregs of masochism still remaining from my illness. I lay there lost in time and space, thoughts mixed but shifting from unconsummated love and romance with Neil, to counting the scars on my arms left from attempts at suicide, or were they perhaps cries for help? I predictably gave up the task as pointless around the one hundred and fifty mark. I had long been aware of a fine line between madness and as I was today. I considered Justin who had saved my life, the hell I had put him through for years and the thousands of occasions I had scrutinised why he had given hundreds of hours of his time for free to nurse me, mind body and soul. 'Are you for real?' I asked him when he turned down the only ability I had of paying. Nothing was for nothing, life had taught me that, there were no exceptions. This geezer thought he was God, 'twas the only explanation, unless he'd got a screw loose, or both. He ran day centres for alcoholics, prescribed drug addicts and substance misusers. I was all three and anorexic to boot. My circulatory system was breaking down and incessant pains racked my stomach and particularly my legs. The local GP sent me to a specialist, both agreed gangrene was a possibility. 'You are in grave danger of losing your left leg,' the words fell on hollow ground, I had at least forty milligrams of Valium inside me at the time and enough wine to dine a group of six. Justin came to me through the only friend I had left - Jacqui Whittaker - a physio employed at The David Lloyd Tennis Club in Middlesex of which I was a member. I only agreed to meet him to get her off my back. At the time it had not fully registered in my addled brain he was my last stopping place on the way to some cemetery or another.

He talked to me as a human being, this was new. No-one had done this for a long time, odd-bod was all I thought as he talked about the wonders of sobriety and how each day in my post drinking drug taking life, would be a revelation of monumental proportions. When he had gone, alone in my bedsit I schemed about how I could be rid of him. Trouble was, all Justin predicted began to come true over the weeks that followed. Little things at first, then more subtle and less predictable adjustments for the good fell into place all because my body was clean of drugs of any sort. I suffered the most horrendous mental aberrations, an instability which promised no end. Yet in between I sampled periods of how it was to be normal, which I recognised only because my foster mother had spoken of them. She did so despite my cynical reaction to each and every word she uttered which I construed as her attempting to spoil my fun, simply because she was jealous. Now of course I knew differently. I shrugged my shoulders and eased myself painfully from my bed and concentrated on the day ahead instead of the past which kept reappearing out of context. 'Normal,' was to ask 'good morning, how are you?' And mean it. To awaken refreshed from a deep sleep each day, rather than regaining consciousness with a hangover and incessant anxiety and panic attacks. Establishing credibility and respect from my fellow man and for people to like me because, basically, I was sober and an O.K. person. This was normal.

Neil had not reciprocated my love. The poor boy had endured my unsolicited attentions and intrusions into his domestic life to such a degree that he was driven to distraction. For my part, my precarious mental condition was now exacerbated by a destructive obsession probably qualifying me as one of Britain's first stalkers. It had all begun at the Red Cross Camp but escalated out of control from the till at Marks and Spencers. I knew where he lived with his parents from the early days and commenced a systematic plan to net my prize. It culminated in an obsession of such monumental proportions and irrationality that, together with my already delicate mental state, sent me completely over the edge. Neil had spurned my approaches at every turn. Over a period of time extending to a year or more, I changed my appearance to match the various women I saw in his company varying from blonde to brunettes. From a size twelve I became a ten and then an eight. I took an interest in theatre after seeing him buy tickets, and bought a crash helmet which I stood holding in many a club or pub after he purchased a motorbike. Slowly I slipped into a state of decadence which with hindsight, I was unaware of thus accepting it as a normal way of life. I had simply never recovered from my adolescent torments and the inadequacies born out of losing my childhood. Terrifyingly, my irrational behaviour was an acceptable way to conduct myself. For me irrationality was ordinary.

I took a Wilkinson Sword razor blade to my wrist in the toilets of a dress shop where I had embarked upon a new career, and cut the main artery.

CHAPTER TEN

ANGIE DIXON AND THE TWILIGHT YEARS

As I walked from the hotel that afternoon and headed towards the shopping centre, I thought a lot about my first attempt at suicide. It was not simply the act itself, it was the actions of people around me during, and in the immediate aftermath, which occupied my thoughts as I walked.

My foster parents sent me a get well card to the hospital. I opened it and my blood ran cold...they had signed it 'from Mr. and Mrs. Barker'. Felicity came to see me. For the life of me I am unable to ascertain precisely how we kept in touch but nevertheless it was so. Trouble was, two of my blood siblings came as well on the same day at exactly the same time, the atmosphere was dreadful. For reasons I am unable to recount, they did not come into my ward which was small with just four beds, it was left for me to sit in the corridor outside where six chairs were strategically placed. One of the other three beds was occupied by a Maltese woman who conjured up imaginings of Cruella De Vill. She and her husband, who visited her regularly, were into witchcraft and sexual perversion. I had decided then, if you were evil those with similar deviances would seek you out. Today I was furious at such a notion.

It took barely ten minutes to walk to the home where Angie Dixon lived. An Irish woman of about sixty answered my knock and said she had no knowledge of her, the only useful bit of information was, she herself had lived there for six years, which told me Angie was long gone. I thanked her for her help, simultaneously apologised for the intrusion and headed back towards the town centre. I had walked barely five yards from her gate when a voice rang out.

'Nikki, Nikki, Nikki Stevens!' My maiden name sounded alien after so many years but I had no hesitation in responding to the voice. It belonged to an extremely fat woman of indeterminable age, beaming all over her face and waddling towards me like an extremely large duck.

'Nikki how lovely to see you, you haven't changed a bit, how do you manage it?' I said all the right things, smiled and grimaced in all the correct places and joined in the conversation valiantly, but twenty minutes later I had not the slightest idea who the dear soul was. I tried to imagine her thinner, blonde, brunette and lopped off as many years as my imagination would allow but to no avail. She was a complete stranger.

'Please come back home with me for tea or coffee,' she implored. Curiosity rather than thirst took me several hundred yards to a house I recognised immediately as the place where an old school friend had lived with her parents.

'Of course, Mummy and Daddy are dead now, but I took on the house.' She prattled on incessantly from one thing to another, I missed it all because I was completely preoccupied putting Catherine Daley, or 'Spindle' as we called her at school, into this enormous carcass. She had been so thin she could have been suffering from malnutrition, slowly I saw bits of the old Catherine and a sudden note of near hysterical exclamation brought me back to the present. 'Do you remember the Maltese Witch who was in hospital with you?' Cruella's apparition materialised in my minds eye.

'God!' I managed. 'She scared me to death.' Spindle went quiet for the first time since shouting my name in the street and nodded in agreement. 'I don't know who was the most evil her, or that bloody foster sister of yours for arranging that ridiculous homecoming party.'

'What on earth do you mean?' I asked truly amazed.

'Well! You had cut a main artery with a razor blade because Neil wouldn't go out with you. Two weeks later you were discharged full of stitches, Felicity hired the village hall together with sandwiches and booked Neil of all people to do the disco, then she stood in the corner grinning like a Cheshire cat for the rest of the night. Evil cow!'

A feeling of genuine indignance swept over me. I knew Felicity and I had our differences, but

I was sure she loved me in her own way, as much as I loved her in mine - or did she? There had been one episode that cast a shadow.

A major family incident, the ramifications of which had lived on, had occurred shortly after our return from Singapore. It came about as a result of my birth mother deciding to have all her family back together again, including her second husband's children, to live in a large house he owned in the country. The proposition was put to me by my foster mother and father together, who had sat me down for a serious discussion, although she did the talking. I remember being quite excited at the prospect and saying I would like to go, but more distinctly my foster mother's expression of devastation and disbelief. She did not know that the attraction for me, was the 'glamour' as I perceived it to be of having lots of brothers and sisters and perhaps even cats and dogs.

The decision was made. A pin could have been heard to drop in my last week at the Barkers. Then the night before I was due to leave, a phone call came saying mad mother had changed her mind. Felicity only ever spoke to me from then on to say, 'You're only here because no-one else wants you,' or words to that effect, and I could not explain I had imagined in my confused mind I wouldn't actually have to leave the Barkers. Perhaps Felicity had not forgiven...

'Do you remember going to the to the Maltese Falcon's house?' Spindle interrupted my thoughts, referring to the woman in the ward I had nicknamed Cruella De Vill. I nodded as she looked at me expectantly. We had been given a drink on arrival and the next thing we remembered was waking up naked, staked out in a star shape, covered in an evil musk-smelling oil with candles burning everywhere. I shuddered at the memory of an awful pain in between my legs and felt sick as I remembered taking a foreign body from deep within. Spindle had freed herself and untied me and we had run for our lives from an apparently empty house. We both agreed it had probably been a narrow escape. Privately, I wondered how such evils, all too often, were attracted to me.

Catherine (I could not somehow bring myself to call her Spindle out loud) and I enjoyed the whole afternoon together, and not only did I delight in our meeting, but also she was able to give me Angie Dixon's new address which was on the other side of town.

That night my thoughts were wholly occupied by my stay with Angie at a time in my life when I could not distinguish between reality and fantasy. Even the warmth and safety of the hotel was little comfort from the memory of those terrible days.

I remembered Angie from school...just. She had found me drunk in a High Street gutter in the early hours of an alcoholic morning, covered in blood and took me home. She had a good heart but was a drug addict, a prostitute and traded both with extremely dangerous people. The timing of my arrival could not have been worse as far as I was concerned, she was in the middle of a war. Money lending on a massive scale was big business on the council housing estates. Someone would borrow ten pounds at five per cent calculated on a daily basis and timed by the clock, would owe ten pounds and fifty pence after twenty-four hours. If it was borrowed against the weekly giro the profit for the 'loan baron' by the end of the week, would be three pounds and fifty pence. Multiply this by fifty people or more, plus much heavier loans and you have a massive profit on the initial investments. Frequently, the week would run into two or three and the usual penalty was to double the rate of interest, effectively meaning the loan was never paid off and the income for the 'loan baron' permanent. Failure to pay would result in damage to property, threats and often terrible beatings. My arrival at Angie's was to coincide with the wrath of a drug-dealer let down on a heroin deal who was also owed loan debts, supposedly collected from the individual borrowers by Angie. Angie was in big trouble...she hadn't got the money.

It was my second night at her house and I was withdrawing from alcohol. Sleep eluded me and I lay sweating, listening to a nearby church clock chiming every quarter hour and then the hour. I had heard eleven, twelve, one, two, I never heard three. Shortly after two thirty I heard voices and then an almighty crash as the front door caved in followed by a stampede of a dozen or so villainous types high on drugs and alcohol.

Angie's screams were terrifying and the sound of her beating was sickening. At first I cowered beneath the bedclothes in the hope I would remain undiscovered, but there was to be no escape. I was still alone in my room at this stage and a quarter of an hour later there seemed no let-up, I wondered how Angie could be surviving and I shook so much it was more like convulsions than fear. Hesitantly, I eased myself from under the bedclothes and moved furtively towards the window, then I stopped - Angie lived on the fourth floor of a block of flats, no escape there. Abruptly, I realised everything had gone quiet and crept towards the source of her suffering. I pushed open the lounge door and the sight that greeted me paralysed every nerve in my body. Angie was naked, kneeling on all fours with a naked man under her performing the conventional sex act. Behind her, on his knees penetrating her anus, was a further character holding an evil looking knife against her head. A third man knelt before her his penis rammed down her throat making her choke - her arms were tied out straight in wing-like fashion to heavy armchairs on either side of her. A further half dozen or so stark naked men of indeterminable age lined up ready to prolong her humiliation - then they spotted me.

The following six hours was a living nightmare tempered only by the fact I was forced to swallow a quantity of drugs of unknown origin. That I was raped constantly, by perpetrators who had sunk lower than any animal with a ferocity and endurance that could only have been fuelled by drink and drugs, is in no doubt. Precisely what occurred during the remainder of the night is mercifully erased from my memory, although the pain and suffering of the ensuing seven or eight days will live forever in the darkness of my tortured psyche. I ached in places, from injurious bestialities no woman should ever have to endure. I vomited continually for several days and my eyesight, inexplicably, had developed an inability to focus properly. Angie, for her part took twenty four hours to regain consciousness, and I even thought at one stage she was dead. A measure of my own physical condition was that despite an overwhelming concern for her, I could not function sufficiently to leave the building and call a doctor. Gradually, over several days, normality was restored. It began with Angie groaning once, then often and struggling around the flat, first on all fours and then in an upright though bent position. She occasionally grunted apologies that I had been involved. Through it all, I lay on the bed knees tightly brought up under my chin and left it only for the bathroom. On the ninth day Angie left to buy some food and I escaped, but only into another calamity.

As I was leaving the flat I glanced through Angie's bedroom door which stood open wide. A large piece of paper with black letters written in felt pen was still bayoneted to the wall with a huge chef's chopping knife. It read:

Debt paid in kind!!

The following day I followed Catherine's instructions to Angie Dixon's new home - she was out. I was glad in an obscure sort of way, my reflective memories had been quite sufficient to satisfy the therapeutic curiosity and my token effort to visit her had left me fulfilled.

CHAPTER ELEVEN

HAYLEY, DAILY

Hayley and I raced at breakneck speed in a powerful sports car, blonde hairs streaming out in the wind almost perfectly horizontal to our upright sitting positions. The brilliant summer sunshine enhanced the highlights of hair and fashion alike, and our laughter was as infectious as it was exhilarated. Unexpectedly, the throb of the car's power unit together with road noise and atmospherics began to fade, and then disappeared altogether. Only the warmth of the sun remained to be joined by the clinking, clattering and vocal sounds of everyday hotel life.

I lay still for a while disturbed by the vivid, vibrant, intensity of the dream, and reconciling myself with the disappointment of the reality of not having a Hayley in my life. Thoughts of her, and any possibilities of her survival, however far-fetched, had disappeared into the back of my mind undoubtedly due to the improbability. Despite being consumed by my journey of remembrance, I was beginning to develop shadows of the past that reflected images of my days with the hippies. The first time I had seen Hayley, peculiar and disturbing reverberations began to register in my memory bank. The prospect that she may have survived and been sold off by evil rather than friendly, helpful Bohemians, was emerging as an alarming and distressing contemplation. I would have been the first to concede that memories of my past seemed as a life lived by someone else. Nonetheless, it was my life and I was personally involved, and I needed to find Hayley. I had to speak to her - I had to find out if she was an adopted child born in February 1972. I knew this would solve nothing as far as law and order, or indeed history were concerned. Neither would it change the intervening years, for sure it would not unite us and this was certainly not my intent. It was not to mend my broken heart, for time had healed the wounds and numbed the maternal instincts that had been so painful long ago. Yet there was a void, an unfilled space in my existence, I had to know if she had survived however fantastic the notion seemed. Today I would try to find her.

As I dressed for the day I smiled and considered how little had changed through the generations with regard to the habits of the city's youth. Twenty years previously we had two main meeting places. One was the Abbey Gardens where wooden benches were in abundance placed in close proximity for the benefit of tourists. At night they were claimed by the young ones meeting in the hope of romance, to show off fashion, motorcycles or even cars, or simply just for the craic. The other venue was a park area where there stood a large ladies and gentlemans toilets, though no lady or gentlemen up to any good went there at night. We called it Bog Park and went there to smoke, drink, and more. Two decades later only the faces had changed, though some looked remarkably familiar and I could not help but wonder if their mums or dads had lingered there with me. I had walked through the Abbey Gardens deliberately going out of my way on at least two evenings during my stay. I had noticed only one real change, and that was a total disregard for my brief presence in their midst as I passed through. In my day we would have gone quiet, stared suspiciously and even passed sarcastic remarks at the poor grown-up victim. I had not revisited 'Bog Park' on this trip, I had doubts as to its value to these emancipated young things who actually seemed to be enjoying themselves far more than we ever did. There was a great deal of music in evidence, dancing and swigging from designer type bottles of alcoholic beverage. Suspiciously fat cigarettes and other objects were passed from one to the other in return for cash, which might have appeared at first glance to the untrained eye like a modern version of pass the parcel.

I left the hotel without breakfast and walked towards the Abbey, wondering where to start my search. As I did so I began to feel ever so slightly stupid at my naivety. I had seen Hayley fewer than half a dozen times in less than a week, and here I was foolishly setting out expecting to find her instantly amongst a population of eighty thousand people. If that was not sufficiently far-fetched I was then going to march up to her and ask if she had been adopted, was born under Aquarius or Pisces with a February birthday, and had an uncle or auntie who wore lots of beads. I sank down on a seat in a bus shelter and again considered going home.

* * * * * * * * * * *

My meanderings began again and I thought of the day I had left Angie's after recovering from the night of terror. I recalled, out of desperation deciding to go back to my birth mother, with whom I had kept occasional contact but barely knew, to ask if she would put me up. She was living just thirty miles away in Southampton, and I made the decision to leave with a flourish I perceived to be symbolic, due to the major effect it was bound to have on the lives of everyone around me.

I made several dozen telephone calls telling all and sundry, who in reality couldn't have cared less, that I was going to leave town and kill myself. For Miss Lewis, my former teacher whom I still idolized, I wrote a letter full of heartbreak, graphically describing my life of torment, and included my intention to leave town on the 11a.m. train and jump from a speeding carriage.

I recalled as vividly as though it were yesterday, my heroine arriving at breakneck speed down the road leading to the railway station after a three mile ride. Her skirts were blowing in the wind, her ancient bicycle creaking under the strain. I was sat outside the building on a bench, an hour to kill before the train arrived, and watched entranced as Miss Lewis raced in my direction waving a white book. She screeched to a halt, jumped from the machine and ran breathlessly sitting down with a huge bump beside me. She hugged me tightly, began to speak to me spiritually, 'bless this child' and finally stood over me reciting a prayer and handed me the white book - a Holy Bible decorated in white with gold lettering. She sat with me until my train arrived and we waved until she was the size of a pin in the distance.

I stood at the door of the home my mother shared with her second husband Tommy, and my request for refuge hung in the air like a bad smell. It was probably only fifteen seconds, but it felt an eternity as she seemed to be deciding whether or not I was one of the seven she had given birth to. Then without warning she stood back and opened the door.

Tommy was a really nice man who deserved better than my mad mother, although given her suffering mainly at the hands of Arthur, perhaps this is somewhat unfair. Additionally, because of her existence with him, she was under treatment from her doctor who had prescribed 10 mg of Diazepam four times daily. Some ten years AA (after Arthur), she was tragically hooked on this Benzodiazepine or hypnotic drug better known as

Valium, which has the most horrendous with-drawal ramifications. Doctors handed them out like Smarties in the sixties, when it was known as a saviour drug for those depressed or anxious. It had now fallen to me as part of my job, to deal with some of the casualties at my place of work. In my view there is no such thing as a quick detox from Valium. The quicker the victim is weaned off the more chance there is of them slipping back, and those who successfully stay off, can suffer the most vile flashback withdrawal symptoms for as much as five years or more later. A few, doped up to the eyeballs like my mother, can walk around like zombies and be guilty of the most outrageous mood swings. I was victim of at least one of these that I will never forget and could easily have been fatal. I am left in no doubt retrospectively, that Tommy saved my life.

Mother had eventually welcomed me in, and the first few days were so idyllic I had seriously begun to question all the anger of a lifetime rooted in her giving me away. I would help with the housework during the morning and we would break it up with morning coffee at eleven a.m. Mother would pop her tablet and soon began to offer one to me, which I swallowed eagerly in the absence of alcohol. In due course, and naturally more quickly than would be the norm, she ran out of her supply and went to the GP for a repeat pre-scription. He duly refused on the basis that she had doubled her dose, informing her that she could not have a further supply for at least a week

- she returned home face as black as thunder. By the following morning she was climbing the walls in mental anguish at the loss of the drug, screaming obscenities at Tommy and then me with increasing ferocity. Then, inexplicably, she went quiet and retreated to the kitchen. Suddenly, without a single word of warning, the kitchen door leading to the lounge where I was standing with Tommy burst open, and Mother, with an expression resembling Norman Bates in Psycho, lunged through it holding a wicked looking carving knife. Arm stretched out in front of her, she charged at speed towards me screaming that I had stolen tablets from her handbag. Both Tommy and I were frozen to the spot by the suddenness of her action, but thankfully for me he recovered first. Flinging out an arm, he thrust me with all his might across the room where I landed in a heap banging my head on the wall. Almost in one movement he grabbed Mother's wrist which held the knife and wrestling her to the floor, held her down with extreme difficulty until the madness subsided. It took several minutes for me to recover - shakily I grabbed my few belongings and fled the house, Mother's curses still ringing in my ears.

'Do you want a bus or not?' The driver/conductor awakened me from my mother's world and a quick glance reminded me I was still sat in the bus shelter. 'No, sorry, I'll get the next one.' He drove off eyes raised to the heavens.

During the two days and nights that followed I spent practically every waking hour searching for the little blonde livewire I had dubbed Hayley. I carried a small photo in my purse, which had been taken when I was around about the same age as she was now, and I looked at it constantly. The more I did so, the more I became convinced Hayley had lived and I was aware it was becoming an obsession.

On the next day of my search I decided towards teatime that tonight I would not have a hotel meal and instead would do something simple. It was the smell of freshly baked bread coming from a supermarket bakery that gave me the idea. Oh! How I do love hot crusty rolls and lashings of butter. As I headed quickly towards the delicatessen counter the frustrations of my fruitless search had receded and were even temporarily forgotten such was my yearning. My weight passed quickly from the sole of one foot to the other as I stood impatiently in the queue. All of a sudden I was rooted to the spot. There in the middle aisle, looking ridiculous in a Sainsbury's hat and surrounded by pork pies, stood Hayley.

The hot rolls and butter forgotten, I reversed to another section out of sight so I could collect myself. It took several minutes. I had been rehearsing for days precisely what I would say, but now faced by the reality of seeing her I struggled to recall even a single word. Eventually, I pulled myself together and walked up to her.

'Excuse me, could you tell me....?' My voice trailed off, I was looking beyond her and out through the plate glass window at the English

Heritage protected horse trough. Hayley was stood where she had been born.

'Here you are, sit down, would you like a glass of water?' Hayley's accent was West Country as mine had once been and her face showed genuine concern. 'No, I'll be fine, you're very kind!' The anxious expression on her face relaxed and she smiled instead and said, 'I thought you were going to faint.' Then she laughed and I laughed too. I stood up feeling better and said without thinking, 'Haven't I seen you somewhere before?'

Hayley looked long and hard and then shook her head. 'No, I don't think so, although you do look familiar.' I scrutinised every inch of her face and saw my family's distinguishing features around the eyebrows and hairline. I was now calm and in complete control, it had become a normal chat between two people simply being polite.

'Yes you look familiar too,' I said warmly. 'I went to school here myself thirty years ago, perhaps I knew your mum and dad.'

'You may have done, but then you would be one up on me because I don't know them. You see I was adopted.'

My heart pounded in my chest but I stayed calm and said only, 'Well it's their loss!' She just smiled. 'Did you not bother to find them?' I enquired.

'Nope! I really don't give a shit.' Hayley did not look like me when she was angry, she reminded me of Justin and for sure he was not connected, suddenly I was not so sure anymore. No matter how hard I tried, now I could no longer see my mother or brother in her at all. I was experiencing disappointment but the conversation continued unabated. She laughed a lot as the subject changed from her job to her boyfriend and his new sports car, and the rows they were getting into for driving too fast and staying out late. The more we chatted the more I became convinced I was mistaken and the less I could see of me in her as a young girl. I began to twist my long blonde hair between my fingers until each tress could turn no more, a habit I had had since childhood. 'Do you always shop in Sainsbury's?'

Hayley's question interrupted my habit and my primary thoughts, and unexpectedly I thought I saw my foster sister in her expression. 'God! This is ridiculous.'

'Pardon?' She looked surprised by my outburst, and collecting myself quickly I explained I was now too late for an appointment I'd had, but didn't give a shit either. We both laughed together loudly.

'Oh well I must go,' I said finally. 'I do hope all goes well with you and your boyfriend. Be careful in that car you mentioned, you have the rest of your lives ahead of you.'

'Yes we will, you too. By the way I'm Sally what's your name?' 'Nikki.' I said and with a wave walked away.

I had reached the exit when I realised I had not picked up my handbag, quickly I retraced my steps. Hayley who was Sally stood exactly where I had left her, my handbag on the floor unnoticed by her side.

'I'd lose my head if it wasn't screwed on,' I joked as I retrieved it. 'By the way, what's your birth sign?'

Hayley looked thoughtful for a moment and then said. 'Well, it's a bit complicated. You see I don't really know, but I've always celebrated it on Valentines Day.' I wished her well once more and left the shop. As I walked along the pavement in front of the window adorned with special offers and discounts for everything from soap to lamb chops, my eyes searched for one last look. She was where I left her, though now sat on a box of tins gazing thoughtfully into space, twisting a long tress of blonde hair until it could go no further.

CHAPTER TWELVE

KILLER FATHER ARTHUR

After leaving Sainsbury's I felt strangely at ease - not an emotion I was altogether familiar with. I settled on a seat in the Abbey churchyard and absorbed the summer sunshine in thoughtful mood.

My meeting with Sally had told me little and solved nothing, yet I was inexplicably comforted. It was as though, through our short time together, I had been able to address the trauma I had previously kept hidden from even my closest friend. Perversely I had never denied having a child, on the contrary I had been quite open about it and told friends (and the world and his wife when I had been drinking) my baby had been adopted by a wealthy family. The terrible reality was, through alcohol and drugs my memory retained only mystery and contradiction. Yet delusion may well have been fact.

I recalled affectionately, though with some guilt, my days out with the Zipoli children when I weaved my web of fantasy around being their mother. Little Samantha, whom I met in the park when aged eight, had stayed in occasional touch over the years and accepted my story that the children had been adopted. She had been a constant reminder of the lie I had lived. Had her presence not been fairly regular thus providing a witness to their existence, I pondered on whether I would have changed my tale, though my gut feeling was the truth would have been even more fantastic.

Immediately upon leaving my knife wielding mother's home, I had bumped into Phyllis Dailey who had been a year ahead of me at school. She was strikingly beautiful and outstandingly successful with members of the opposite sex, we greeted each other like long lost friends.

'Where are you off to then?' was her eventual question, and I responded along the lines of having nowhere to go. 'Well you'd better come home with me then.' I went for a night and stayed twelve months.

By this time I was drinking large amounts of alcohol and popping tablets on a regular basis, and not surprisingly much of the time is a blur in my memory. Actual events of the previous twelve months, and much of the subsequent three years, is a jumble of hazy recollections and the odd vivid and unforgettable nightmarish incident. Phyllis for example had a deep rooted problem the nature of which remains unclear to this day. Despite my professional experience in the area of psychology and the fact she remains a close friend, I have never got to the bottom of it and it remains an enigma. Phyllis was into body mutilation to such a degree, that I have sat with her in a room consumed by nausea and terror with blood pouring everywhere and lumps of flesh hanging like meat in a butchers shop. Sometimes she would return home with a black eye, at other times I would catch her accidentally getting out of the shower and see deep bruising all over her body. For someone so exceptionally pretty it was sad to see her desecrate her beautiful body, not just with knives and razor blades, but also with extensive tattooing in the name of art.

Further examples of past torments rearing their ugly heads were to be found in both our existences. With horrendous regularity, and sometimes in unison, we would awake screaming in the dead of night soaked in sweat and shaking from some unseen horror. We had very little money and lived on an almost starvation diet, despite this we nearly always had cigarettes and alcohol on tap. One outstanding recollection of this period and for reasons I cannot recall, is the fact I was terrified of Phyllis. My eventual departure came about when her electric iron gave up the ghost while I was using it. She flew into a rage and ordered me out of the house to get a new one, and not to return until I had. Pathetically, yet perhaps significantly linked to my mental state at the time, I proceeded to knock on doors street after street asking if they had an old iron they did not want. Nothing was forthcoming and I crept back in the middle of the night to retrieve my clothes, left the key on the mantle shelf and trudged off to nowhere.

I walked the streets that night and nodded off for only a minute or so on a bench or bus shelter seat. The following day I trekked from pub to pub in search of anyone who might be sympathetic; I found Father Arthur.

He was as drunk as a skunk, and although we had met only occasionally over the years and were therefore hardly bosom buddies, he knew who I was and always made an outrageous fuss of me. I recall he would sit me on the counter at his local pub announcing loudly I was his beautiful daughter. I was always yearning to be loved and thought it was wonderful. That Arthur hadn't got a tooth in his head, was always drunk and most of the onlookers were as pissed as he was and probably frightened of him, was somehow lost on me. It had been my intention as a last resort to call on Hannah, the most receptive of my sisters, to see if she could put me up for a while. Arthur would hear none of it. 'You will stay with me,' he thundered. This was the last thing I really wanted to do, although I knew not why and tried everything I could think of to wriggle out of it, eventually I agreed to a compromise - a cup of tea at his flat.

Arthur never intended to let me out of his flat that night and it was never his intention to make me a cup of tea. No sooner was the front door closed, than he locked it and told me I could have the spare bedroom previously occupied by my step sister, a daughter by his third wife. I went in and closed the door. At once it came crashing open. He stood in front of me swaying slightly in his drunken state and mumbled over and over again how alike I was to my mother Veronica. I recalled the horror of what I had perceived as love and attention at his hands when I was an infant and it crossed my mind perhaps he singled me out rather than any of the others, because I so resembled his wife. 'Take off your clothes.' His voice had suddenly become calm and the expression on his face like stone. I refused loudly and attempted to pass by him and escape through the door. He pushed me back into the room roughly; 'Strip!' The single word rang out accentuating the emptiness of the room, and all the fear of a lifetimes abomination swept over me in a single moment. Hands shaking I began to obey, struggling with buttons and attempting a token resistance by reminding him I was his daughter, not my mother. He left the room and I thought for a moment my pleas and perhaps even virtue had prevailed. Arthur re-entered and shoved a cotton nightdress into my hands. 'Put it on!' he ordered. Trembling, I did as bid and all the time he just watched, occasionally licking his lips like a dog anticipating a bone. Finally I was finished and stood shivering partly through cold, mainly through fear and in anticipation of my fate.

'You can sleep in my bed,' he said unexpectedly, and I looked up from the floor enquiringly.

'Why would I want to do that?' My voice sounded far away.

'Because we're going to make love!' My heart

sank to a low difficult to describe. The whole experience seemed unreal, and to hear a man who said 'fuck' every other word talk about 'making love', was surreal.

'You're not going to put a finger on me or I'll scream the roof off.' I was desperate - he was still calm. He left the room again but returned almost immediately holding a wicked looking kitchen knife. 'You'll do as you're told or I cut your fucking throat. I've killed once and got away with it, and I can do it again.' The calmness was gone and saliva dripped from his mouth as he spat out the words and he had me convinced. 'I pushed that drunken cow Bridie off the balcony, no-one knew the truth.'

I never knew his second wife, but Arthur had hinted during previous drunken moments there was mystery surrounding her death. He had usually followed the insinuations with a leering smile. He was calm again, but there was a hiss in his voice and the almost controlled countenance was hauntingly similar to insane murderers I had seen portrayed in drama movies. Abruptly, he grabbed me in a headlock and I felt the cold steel across my throat as he dragged me screaming to his room. I flew through the air and landed on the bed banging the side of my face on the headboard. He knelt with one knee on the bed and the point of the knife at my throat and undid his belt, unzipped his trousers and fell heavily on top of me. I felt a knee roughly in my crotch, then penetration and I sobbed and sobbed in pain and for reasons I cannot reasonably explain - shame. Despite the knife I felt there was something I could have done. In a bizarre metamorphosis, I saw myself as the guilty one who had ensnared my poor innocent father when I was a baby, into doing things to me he had not done to my sisters or any of his other children. I had perpetrated the very same crime against Auntie Joan and Billy Goat Gruff, and even the lovely innocent Paul on board the Chitral had not escaped. I was an evil that should be exterminated and I deserved to die... the outrage ended with a crashing fist to the jaw.

I was relieved when I awoke alone. I could hear Arthur moving about in the kitchen and I was just about to slip out of bed, when the door opened and he entered holding a tray containing tea and a fried breakfast.

'Morning!' he said cheerily. 'I've brought you something to eat!'

'I-I need to go to the toilet,' I stammered. He made no effort to stop me, and once inside I locked the door and considered my options furiously. I recalled almost immediately the bathroom door being the first on the left when you entered the flat through the front door...could this be my chance? Without further thought I opened the bathroom door, twisted the handle on the outside door and made good my escape. I was convinced I was flee-ing for my life and was two floors down before I remembered I was still in the cotton nightie and nothing else. I pounded hysterically on the nearest door to me, a startled woman opened it allowing me to push past her and I babbled out my story to her and an even more astonished husband. 'I was Arthur's daughter from upstairs, he had raped me etc etc etc.' No sooner had I finished there was a soft tap on the door, the lady answered and there stood Arthur, meek and mild holding a neatly folded pile of my clothes. 'I've just brought the daughter's clothes down, she's a bit strange and very excitable you know.' The pile was passed to me and I went without asking to a back room and got dressed. When I emerged Arthur had gone. 'Is there anything we can do?' The man's voice tailed off as his wife pulled at his sleeve. I decided I would not want to be Arthur's neighbour either with all the drunken ramifications of noise and violence. 'No, just call me a cab if you don't mind.' I sat down and waited.

The car dropped me off at my sister Hannah's and I burst into tears which streamed down my face. 'Dad's raped me.' I screamed. Hannah was as calm as a cucumber. 'Don't be so bloody silly, what's come over you?' 'I'm telling you the truth,' I countered. 'Please help me, will you call the police?' Hannah looked appalled. 'Look, you're all upset, you know our Dad wouldn't do anything like that, go and have a bath and you'll feel better afterwards.' I took the bath and I did calm down, but not before I had scrubbed every inch of my flesh until it was almost raw. I felt defiled, but more than that, I experienced total isolation as if I was a condemned man about to be executed for a crime I had not committed. My soul was crying for help to a God who would not listen while living in a world that did not care. It was the ultimate sensation of helplessness. I dried myself slowly with a feeling of utter despair enveloping my past and present and I was quite unable to see any future. The only emotion I could feel was one of complete mental and physical desolation.

* * * * * * * * * * *

The sun shining down onto the Abbey churchyard disappeared behind a cloud and the suddenness brought me back to the present. I was glad. These were memories I had to deal with on an ongoing basis but they had receded over the previous few years and I had no desire to stimulate them. I allowed myself to dwell for a few moments on what had happened next. I had gone alone to a police station in the next town and endured a humiliation only marginally less painful than the one which had led me there. The officers were animals and I had hated the police ever since. I was given a four hour grilling by six different uniformed men, two had travelled from Arthur's local police station. It was years later I learned that a policewoman should have been present and at least a degree of kindness afforded - I received neither. My father when interviewed, apparently told them I was a bad lot, totally promiscuous and had deep rooted mental problems. Several officers who knew him as a drunk and petty villain came down firmly on his side saying it was not in his character to do such a thing. The sergeant in charge informed me I would be torn to pieces by a defence counsel. He spoke roughly saying there was no forensic evidence due to the amount of time that had elapsed before an examination had taken place. Finally, he pushed a piece of paper in front of me retracting my accusations stating it was best all round if I signed it. Even then it was as if fate was trying to influence my final decision - it took three pens before he found one with enough ink in it for me to sign my name.

CHAPTER THIRTEEN

MY THREE EMPTY YEARS

As I left the Abbey churchyard I struggled to assemble in my mind the days and weeks that followed the dreadful rape at the hands of my father. My brain had retained intermittent recollections, though it was obvious I was deeply troubled because from then onwards, until I was twenty years old, is practically a blank. In many respects I now recognise from my professional training, the mind has its own way of dealing with trauma often by blotting out that which is too painful to deal with. When dealing with my psychiatric collapse, I was anxious to put definite recollections in context, and those re-emerging as the years passed in the place where presently only void existed.

This I could recall; I had left the police station and walked to the bus terminus. I had gone into the ladies toilet and was immediately confronted by an old hag cum-bag-lady, who had tried to push a dirty doll into my arms cackling ceaselessly, 'hold my baby, hold my baby.' Nothing further registered apart from wandering from bedsit

Safe haven

Nikki aged six with her brother. A picture especially taken by Social Services for their father who was in prison.

Passport east

Pooh...!
Singapore smells

With Asian friends in Singapore

In the swim

Party dress

Calendar Girl
Pictures: R J Prosser

Married to one of nature's gentlemen. Wedding day picture.

Anorexic alcoholic ... aberration

In coat given by passer-by after a suicide attempt in Portsmouth Harbour.

With the Bishop at her confirmation in 1990

1st anniversary of sobriety. A cake modelled on her favourite teddy bear which survived the childrens home years.

With Charlotte, ready for the open road.

Nikki with Charlotte. "First to really love me."

With former film star Mark Eden, now better known as Alan Bradley, Rita of Coronation Street's ex-husband, and his real-life wife Sue Nichols who plays Audrey Roberts. Also in the picture is Crissy Rock, "Best Actress" at the Berlin Film Festival in Ken Loach's film "Ladybird Ladybird."

(above) with Des O'Connor.
(right) Bradley Walsh.

With author Nick Charles who arrived "Justin time."

Nikki today: Agony Aun to millions on the worl wide web.

Pictures: R J Prosser

to bedsit or digs-to-digs, until I met Adam. He was a married businessman who ran various retail outlets around the docks along the south coast, and he desperately needed a manageress for one of them. I got the job and living accommodation near the docks, although I am not sure in which order. I also became involved in the sleazy world of nude modelling and predictably drank far too much alcohol and took drugs.

Inevitably, Adam and I had an affair. I was desperately in need of a friend, a receptive ear and a comforting word. Someone I could confide in. I really yearned for love but knew I would have to settle for less. Adam was less, much less, but at least he was consistent in his lies and deceit, and necessity persuaded me to believe the bits I wanted to believe. Another of his employees was Corrie, she too was one of life's casualties and provided another ear for me, but in her case I had to do my share of listening. One day stands out particularly as an example of the downside of booze and so-called soft drugs. We organised the staff rota so we had our solitary day off together, and were drinking in some bar or another when one of the regulars came up gloating in a slimy way. 'I sin' your pictures in Fiesta magazine. You both got good tits.'

We looked at each other, first in amazement, then in absolute horror as realization dawned. 'Do you remember that party we went to and couldn't recall a thing when we woke up the next morning?' Corrie's words tailed off and then it was my turn.

'We'll sue them, they can't do that.' I was angry but far from convinced and, as it transpired, with good cause. Vaguely, we put together enough of the night to remind ourselves of meeting a professional photographer who had taken us back to his studios - we went to see him two days later demanding cash - he showed us a waiver we had signed in drunken scrawl giving him permission to do whatever he wanted with the pictures - we slunk away. Adam laughed like a drain.

One day I awoke and knew I was pregnant. Shadows of the past lengthened my depression and brought Hayley back until I swallowed a few cans or bottles of wine, then they were gone. On a sober day Adam gave me two hundred pounds for a termination, I spent the lot on baby clothes edged in pink then miscarried. The pain lasted until I managed a drink, or a tablet. Soon life within me began again by whom I know not, this time it was ended by abortion due to medical complications emanating from damage done at Hayley's birth. One day I regained consciousness with a tattoo on my arm, it looked better, smaller...after a drink.

'You dirty filthy cow!' Blows rained down on my unprotected face and body. A man had returned to explain I had given him gonorrhea. I was grateful to him, I deserved to be hurt. Adam and the job were gone. So was my ability to ever conceive again.

I began to hitch lifts regularly in the hope of being murdered. A killer was wreaking havoc in and around the north of England; the national press nicknamed him the Yorkshire Ripper. I headed north desperately wanting him to visit me and rid the world of my evil and relieve me of the pain. I was beaten up more times than I care to remember, brutally raped into double figures and left stranded once in Leeds, each time I survived, even Peter Sutcliffe was wary of me. I began to mutilate my arms on a regular basis. The sight of my blood flowing gently away was beautiful as the skin parted exposing veins, I felt an exhilaration and peace rare in my private world, and I was glad. I never went far without a Wilkinson Sword razor blade. One night I sat on a kerbstone, feet in the gutter, slicing flesh from my arms and bleeding profusely. 'You need a friend.' The voice was soft, the owner female though she was built like a gorilla. It was unkind to say it but she had an ape-like figure and hair grew prolifically narrowing the amount of face visible to the world. She looked grotesque but sounded kind, I followed her to a house on the edge of town. She bandaged my arms, put me to bed, then lay on me so I could not move and forced her head between my legs. I found fear, an emotion not often felt, fought myself free and escaped bleeding into the night.

I telephoned Adam and somehow got past his wife. He came out and installed me in a flat above one of his shops, I had no way of knowing but life was about to change for me forever. A few hundred miles away in Bilbao Peter de Villiers a South African with a heart as big as a bucket was boarding a small passenger liner, the Swedish Lloyd Motor Vessel 'Patricia'. The following morning he walked into my life and remains to this day; although our relationship is not as straightforward as it sounds.

CHAPTER FOURTEEN

de TIME

Despite the bitter memories, I had actually enjoyed the time I spent sitting in the Abbey churchyard. Strangely, the human psyche frequently prefers to retain just the good times, and occasionally I had to struggle quite hard to resurrect the awful bits. In my own mind I knew I would never return on this kind of mission again, and my commitment was such it was vital to establish what had happened and where, in order to retrace my steps accurately. The trip had been strongly recommended by Justin who extolled the virtue of burying ghosts as, 'probably the most important steps I would ever take,' in my new alcohol and drug free life. As with everything else, I followed his instructions to the letter. He had told me to go back and visit each location where the dreadful events had taken place. To sit in the summer sunshine and observe how harmless, inoffensive and innocent the places were that had once held such terror. He told me a story of a former prisoner of war of the Japanese who had spent a year in a cell so small he could not lay out in a straight line. The poor man had placed his head each day by a ventilation grille and watched a colony of ants going to and fro about their business. He thought of them as his only friends. His vision for the future was that one day he would return with a wife he had not yet met and children hitherto unborn. Perhaps it would be as a tourist or in an educational capacity, then he could carry forever the message of peace as an ambassador to a free world. The fantasy helped him survive the terrors and years later he did return with his family to see his cell again. It was being used as a broom cupboard, the door left permanently open, the ants still used the grille, he never had nightmares again.

Justin was right, I knew he would be, nevertheless I couldn't help but wonder if someone or something was on his side. 'Sit in the summer sunshine and observe how harmless, inoffensive and innocent places are that had once held such terror.' He had spoken with sincerity and utter conviction. I laughed to myself, even the British weather took him seriously, the sun had shone non-stop for a week.

I kicked a hamburger carton aimlessly as I walked, and thought of Peter de Villiers. Adam had roused me from my sleep above the shop and I had helped him during a busy morning behind the counter. He could not understand why I had so many hang-ups, why in particular I self-mutilated. He had dressed my arms with stock from the shop and I tried to explain, but it made no sense. I didn't really know myself and years later it would take Justin two years to explain it to me: accurate assessment had taken him a lifetime to learn.

My first customer after lunch was Peter. He was tall, dark, handsome and seemingly rich. He had a top job with South African Airways, a super sports car and a detached house in a secluded avenue near Heathrow Airport, and he wanted me to go out on a date. I nodded, three months later we were married.

Of course nothing is ever quite what it seems and Peter de Villiers' persona was inspired and fuelled by alcohol. The house was rented, the car did not stand up when closely scrutinized and every month, a week before the salary cheque was due, we were broke. Nonetheless, immediately after our wedding we flew to South Africa's Orange Free State to meet my new in-laws in a little village called Hennenman. Back in England we had left Samantha house-sitting, true to her word as an eight year old, she had presented herself on my doorstep on the occasion of her sixteenth birthday. We had been in constant touch by post over the years, with many meetings thrown in. Nevertheless, it was still a shock when she arrived on our doorstep with a single suitcase.

As soon as Peter told me of his intention to honeymoon in the country of his birth, I had collected all the relevant literature I could lay my hands on from travel shops, the South African tourist board and all good book shops who had anything however remote, on the route we were taking and the country itself. They told me amongst endless information that it was a tourists dream and truly the adventure of a lifetime.

South Africa's population had gathered from all over the universe although they are predominantly from Africa itself. Nevertheless few of the original inhabitants, the hunter-gatherer San, remain today. The evidence of their existence over many centuries is available for everyone to see as a result of rock paintings surviving throughout the ages. Tourists, I was told, could actually meet the San at Kagga Kamma (translated Place of the San) which is north of Cape Town in the Cedarberg. This is an area protected for the benefit of the Kalahari San, where they hunt and earn money selling handmade artworks. Their private lives and residences are hidden from the prying eyes of tourists. However, a central meeting point for the benefit of sightseers and the San's commercial activities has been established.

Overwhelmingly, the vast majority of the South African population are black Africans who are fiercely proud of their roots. This group moved from Central Africa's lakeland region and occupy areas all over the country. The different tribes fascinated me and I read over and over again the wonders I was about to see.

In modern day the tribal area of the Xhosa falls generally within the Eastern Cape Province. The Zulus originate from the province of KwaZulu Natal, the Ndebele from Mpumalanga, the South Sotho from the Free State, North Sotho from the

Northern Province, Tswana from the North-West Province, the Venda the Northern Province, Shangaan from Mpumalanga and nearly all the Swazi from areas of KwaZulu Natal and Mpumalanga from the Swaziland borders.

These groups have blended together in urban areas, where they have adopted a western-ised way of life, yet in the rural areas they remain faithful and still practice traditions.

My imagination ran wild as I drank glass after glass of white wine and speculated on the forthcoming trip. I had not travelled far since returning from Singapore and I fantasised my own involvement in the frenetic exhibition of the Zulus in dance, and watched Michael Caine in 'Zulu' at least twice. I saw myself visiting the Ndebele's brightly painted houses and wearing the heavy bronze rings around arms and legs which were seen as a married woman's privilege within the tribe. I loved the comical hats and brightly coloured blankets worn as clothing by the Sotho and marvelled at the initiation ceremonies of the Venda. I imagined being deliberately scarred as a female member of a tribe to deter Arab slave traders...

All through the bottom of a glass, aided and abetted by Samantha.

* * * * * * * * * * * *

The reality was somewhat different. We had a terrible row on the plane, I threw his ring on the floor and it took two attendants, Peter on all fours and an American tourist travelling the world, to find it. Then I refused to put it back on, succumbing only when someone sent over a bottle of spirits especially for me!!

Peter's mother took an instant dislike to me, and it showed in a way that became even more pronounced when the plaster I had put over my tattoos came off in the swimming pool. Looking back, I think his father probably took pity on me and I loved him for it. Without doubt some of his mother's attitude was due to the fact we arrived completely unannounced. In my defence, I had endured the most horrendous train journey from Johannesburg to Hennenman, which is situated near to Welkom, famous for goldmining. It had taken six hours to travel the distance in an airless, aged, dusty, packed carriage in temperatures exceeding 90 Fahrenheit, and all after a fifteen hour delayed flight from London's Heathrow. Thankfully, there was plenty of alcohol available which I thought helped deaden my discomfort. Instead it caused the personality disorder which in reality created much bad feeling upon our arrival and alienated me even more from my mother-in-law. For sure it robbed me forever of the majority of recollections of the trip, although one cultural difference that touched me will live with me for the rest of my life. Peter took me to the post office to mail some letters and I saw first hand the humiliating, and for me, embarrassing side of apartheid. I went in first and stood in a queue with black

Africans and was tugged by the sleeve into a second queue comprising of white people only. Two large signs stood in prominent positions demanding segregation, people of all races were looking at me, I sobered up instantaneously and stared at the floor in shame both for me and the human race.

Our marriage was doomed from the beginning. Alcohol was the prime destructive element for this, but a lifetime of physical and sexual abuse was about to prevent me reciprocating what would be fundamentally and socially accepted as normal consummate lovemaking between newly weds. Peter was the first man in my life who did not belong to someone else, or who was not a one-night stand following a drunken binge. I interpreted his gentle approach as a sign he had changed his mind about me and did not really fancy me after all. During the first six weeks of our marriage he did not beat me up once, and as far as I was concerned this was confirmation of a loveless marriage. I did everything I could possibly think of to provoke him into violence therefore confirming an atom of love for me, without success. We flew back from South Africa with me for the most part in sullen silence, alcohol perking me up in short bursts, only to plunge me back into the depths of despair as I overdid it. We rowed about his mother's obvious dislike for me and just about anything else I could find wrong to use as ammunition. The poor man was driven to distraction, and how he resisted throttling me is a tribute to his tolerance and proof positive that alcohol does different things to different people. It certainly had a quite different effect on him than it did on me.

Two months after our return from South Africa, Peter lost his job with South African Airways due to his drinking. One week later, in order to supplement his unemployment benefit, I became a chambermaid and Samantha threw in a few pounds as a barmaid.

CHAPTER FIFTEEN

INTRODUCING JODI

'You go first, I'm not in any hurry....' Small, dark-haired and petite, the young-looking thirtysome-thing smiled a beautiful smile that lit up the whole of her face. Her eyes seemed to dance and she cocked her head from one inquisitive angle to another chattering incessantly.

'...and it's really been a quite enjoyable stay and I shall definitely come again.' I agreed. Although my visit had brought pain, the hotel was exemplary.

During our brief conversation, which had been surprisingly one sided given my own chatter-box tendencies, we had negotiated the queue for the lift, the lift ride itself, and the stroll along the corridor to our rooms which were separated only by the width of the passage.

'Are you eating alone, because if you are per-haps I could join you? By the way I'm Jodi Fisher!' She held out a hand and I shook it gently. I thought she may have held on for a second or two longer than was necessary, although it could have been my imagination. A little taken aback, despite my worldliness I said: 'That would be nice, give me a knock when you are ready.'

I would have been the first to admit my sexuality was confused, but at that precise moment there were echoes of Jane Cartwright's mysterious kiss on the school tennis courts, and other even less fathomable reflections.

We ate Chinese and Jodi was fascinated by my expert use of chopsticks. I tried to teach her, and we laughed like a couple of schoolgirls as food ended up just about everywhere except where it should. Eventually I owned up to my years in Singapore where I had learned the art from experts, and we became a little sombre as we discussed times gone by in our respective lives. Jodi had lost out in love many times and I confessed to being unsure of the definition of love - period.

'C'mon, cheer up' she said. 'Let's go downtown and catch the late movie at the cinema.'

We bought loads of chocolate and two enormous boxes of hot popcorn which I would have never bought under normal circumstances, and sat close. Then we held hands and the whole double-bill seemed to last but a few minutes.

Back at the hotel we went to Jodi's room and chatted into the early hours and she confided she was abused as a child. 'He was a friend of the family and I thought it was nice and he loved me,' she confided. Justin had been right again. Abusers were also confidence tricksters in so many, many cases. I had heard it said countless times during my work over the years, and here it was again rearing its ugly head during a delightful social evening. Somewhat surprisingly I did not feel immediately inclined to swap experiences in any depth, although I did acknowledge a mutual experience. Jodi did not press me and I had no desire for the minutiae. Her next statement however, touched a nerve and I found myself nodding furiously even before she had finished speaking. She said: 'When I realised where he was coming from and that far from loving me he was a dirty old man, I just wanted him dead.' Despite my emphatic agreement on the day, my own feelings on this issue of course had been a rollercoaster ride.

I remembered how I wanted Auntie Joan and Billy Gruff dead when the same realisation had hit me. One night, when very drunk, I actually hatched a plan to revisit my father and spike his drink with a deadly drug overdose - fortunately, alcohol was doing the planning. "Chitral Paul" on the other hand, had taken longer to hate.

'I'm glad I didn't do anything silly.' Jodie went deadly serious. 'Did you read about a man called Sean Sellers who is on Death Row in Oklahoma State Penitentiary?' I shook my head. 'He was the son of an alcoholic father, and a mother who should have still been at school. They were divorced when he was three and he was farmed out to relatives. By the time he was sixteen he had moved thirty odd times!' Jodi tucked her feet up underneath her as she sat, and took a deep breath. 'Almost from the beginning of his life he had been abused dreadfully and humiliated by his mother, grandfather and an uncle. He was so mentally disturbed by the abuse, he was regularly wetting the bed when he was twelve and made to wear nappies. If he did it two nights in a row he was forced to wear a dirty nappy on his head all day long.

'Violence was part of everyday life, and one of his tormentors tried to teach him to kill animals by stepping on their heads and pulling their legs apart. He was called names because he couldn't do it. Not surprisingly he became withdrawn and completely isolated in a world of his own. Do you want a glass of coke?'

I stared at her for fully ten seconds unable to break the spell the story had created. 'Well?' she repeated. 'Yes, yes please, that would be great.' Jodi poured from a large bottle and continued her story.

'Well, he had been hearing voices in his head from an early age and was a manic depressive - one minute as high as a kite the next in the depths of despair. There is little doubt he was sexually abused over a long period, and finally became obsessed with good and evil because he didn't know the difference. By the time he was fifteen years of age he was practising Satanism daily and drinking his own blood, quantities of which he kept in his fridge. He drank too much alcohol and took amphetamines to excess, all this culminated in violent dreams where he killed members of his family.'

Jodi took a deep breath and a long drink of coke and this time I shifted positions, and waited for her to continue, enthralled but horrified by this incredible story. She swept her hair back with both hands and carried on.

'He drank, and took pills to keep himself awake so as to avoid the nightmares, and after a couple of weeks without sleep he flipped and shot his mother and stepfather in their bed. He admitted the crime and also a murder committed some six months previously in Oklahoma City. Frankly, I think he was quite mad at the time, driven by a lifetime of abuse and substance and chemical misuse which he used to block the turmoil out of his mind.'

'What happened next?' I squirmed, suddenly feeling uncomfortable and wondered how many other poor kids had suffered like Sean Sellers without crossing the slender line into insanity. I pondered on how much like Russian Roulette drink and drugs could become and speculated on how close I might have got to having a bullet in the barrel.

'If everything went according to plan he died today by lethal injection. I suppose you could say in one way they will have executed a child, because he was only sixteen when sentenced to death. There but for the grace of God go I.' Jodi's voice was a whisper. I was stunned!

I suddenly felt very humble, and even guilty for making such a fuss over the relatively easy time I'd had in comparison and said so out loud.

'Don't be bloody stupid.' Jodi was angry and it shook me momentarily. 'Yes you're right.' I said. Everything is relative, but thank God we weren't born in America with all those bloody guns about.' We managed to laugh...

Then we awoke at daybreak... in each others arms.

CHAPTER SIXTEEN

JODI PLUS ONE

We spent the following day together and I began to open up and told of my marriage to Peter. For me it had been a very sad and extremely sombre experience, Jodi was in fits of laughter. At one stage she had to sit down on a grassy bank because her legs would not hold her. She rocked to-and-fro and told me later that the comical look on my face in reaction to her mirth was almost as funny as the story.

I described our financial plight once Peter had lost his job at S.A. Airways through drinking, and how I got a job at the hotel as a chambermaid.

'We had to work in pairs and on my first day I was put with a woman who was twenty years older than me called Anne.' I chortled. 'She was a lovely lady and I'm still close to her to this day, but she was enormously overweight. She had such a job lifting and carrying and negotiating stairs I did most of the work for her. We'd only been working together for a couple of weeks when we were propositioned by a Chinaman who was on a business trip.'

'Hue like rumpty-tumpty free in bed?' said the Chinaman in broken English. I described Anne in detail looking at the poor little chap who was only about five feet tall and told how my imagination ran riot. Jodi laughed and I paused before continuing.

'Well!' I said. 'The very thought of Anne on top of him made me crease up, and neither of us answered immediately, then suddenly he started offering us money.'

'Hue get fiffy pouns,' he offered. 'That was a weeks pay for both of us.' I pointed out somewhat indignantly to the helpless Jodi. Anne just burst out laughing, more at the absurdity of the financial equation than anything else. Then the little chap shouted 'Hokay, I pay wun hunrid.'

Jodi obviously liked my Chinese impression and I waited impatiently for her to stop giggling before carrying on.

'Well, the Chinaman seemed mortified that we might have thought he was unable to pay the going rate and he was jumping from one foot to another in eager anticipation. I've got to be honest I was all for it, and more intimidated at the prospect of performing with Anne than any inhibition created by the Chinaman. I pulled her to one side and pointed out it would be easy money, but she was adamant. Of course my reasoning was influenced by the fact I was full of Valium and drinking at least three bottles of wine a day.' Jodi paused from her laughter at this point, and I studied her tear-stained face.

'You've never had a man have you?' I asked quietly. I looked away not really expecting a reply, then she spoke in a gentle tone I shall always associate with her.

'Not since I was a child.' I bit my lip, a feeling of helplessness in my heart. I decided to try to make her laugh again and recalled demonstratively more of the amusing side of my marriage to Peter exacerbated by the fact we were two alcoholics living together.

'Alcohol affects people differently' I told her. 'But quite often, if a person who is extrovert in their normal state becomes alcoholic, they proceed to lead an even more bizarre existence than an alcoholic who is more introvert to begin with. In our case both Peter and I were extrovert and alcoholic to boot.' Jodi frowned making her eyes squint and I knew she needed an example.

'Look!' I tried hard not to sound impatient as was so vital in my work, and succeeded partially. 'One day I woke up and decided I wanted to be a policewoman and demanded to be taken to Scotland Yard immediately. Peter agreed my presence in the police force would change the shape of British justice and we set off to the Yard. I dread to think what they thought as I made my application at the main reception desk, nevertheless I was treated with the utmost respect. They obviously had a department to deal with folk who just wandered in off the streets, because I was measured by a policewoman and then given an outline of how to apply officially. As soon as an entrance examination was mentioned I got up, said I couldn't possibly do that, and walked out.'

'What on earth did the policewoman say?' Jodi sounded incredulous.

'I really don't know. I left Peter with her gabbling on about nothing, something he was an expert at in his drinking days. A couple of weeks later I decided I wanted to be a bailiff.'

'What?' Jodi shrieked in disbelief. 'Where on earth did you get an idea like that from?' I paused before answering because we must have walked for miles and as I needed refreshment I thought she might too and pointed towards a small cafe.

'Funny you should ask, but I think it might have been a power thing. You see, when I wasn't completely out of it on booze and pills I wanted to be in control of situations, other people and especially me. In some strange way it was as if I was searching for something, almost as if I wanted a mission but could not decide what it was no matter how tirelessly I searched. Most of it was fantasy induced by my addiction, but often it spilled over into reality like the day I went to Scotland Yard. Anyway, I obtained all the relevant information, filled in an application form and after several interviews was offered a position as a trainee based at Stratford in East London.' Jodi shrugged and smiled as she sipped her vanilla milk shake having dumped the straw provided rather messily on the hard-topped table.

'I was assigned to a man for six weeks who

had been a bailiff all his life and the whole period was unforgettable. Our first call came as a result of a woman using superglue to secure herself to the banister at her house in order to defy a compulsory purchase order. What she had done was to empty a whole tube of the stuff on the bottom of the banisters, and then slid down from the top like we did as kids. She arrived at the bottom with a thud and remained there securely glued to the spot. Five hours later, the authorities found London's only female bailiff who naturally enough was considered appropriate, and despatched her to extricate the woman from her trousers. Guess who? ... You got it - me!

'Well, you have never seen such a performance in your entire life. I got almost as tangled up as she was trying to get her out, and at one stage my arm became trapped between her backside and the newel on the bottom of the banister. It took two of my male colleagues to hold her far enough forward for me to free my arm, and I was black and blue for a fortnight. When I got home that night, damn me if I didn't see her on the television news laughing like a drain!'

Jodi finished her milk-shake and we decided to re-order. 'I'll have a strawberry one this time,' she announced to the waitress. 'Make mine a coffee,' I said in turn, adding a guilty 'please' rather hurriedly, as I remembered my days as a waitress.

'God, my life has been a total bore in comparison.' Jodi looked forlorn and I gave her a big squeeze. 'You know as well as I do that these things aren't always funny at the time.' My words had an effect because she began to smile again, and I rattled on.

'But I really must tell you about the goats.' This time there was no reaction just wide eyed expectation.

'As far as I can remember a couple of dozen of them kept getting into a field where they were not welcome. There was something of a feud going on between two neighbouring farmers and it culminated with the one who didn't own the goats taking out a court order against the one who did. Six of us were summoned to evict the goats and I was late arriving. Peter drove me everywhere in our old banger because he was unemployed and had nothing else to do. The night before we had both got paralytic. I always regained consciousness early, dehydrated and with a head I would have liked transplanted - Peter was as if in a coma. By the time I got him back together, I had lost an hour and was expecting a caution from my immediate boss. I was certainly not expecting the sight which greeted me on my arrival. Five very frustrated, dishevelled and desperate looking bailiffs, and two dozen angry looking goats staring at each other across the field they should not have been occupying. I was still quite fortified by the booze overload from the night before and decided to take a closer look at the offending creatures. As I approached I could hear good humoured, but derisory banter coming from my colleagues behind me and could see a deal of suspicion in the eyes of the animals. Undaunted, I walked forward. It was obvious from the geography of the area which field they were supposed to be in, and I could only see one gate that for some reason remained firmly shut. The goats appeared less agitated as I approached and for some reason I began singing softly. To be honest my voice is not all it could be and one or two of them were looking quizzically and making noises back.' Jodi laughed out loud and I paused not wanting her to miss my moment of triumph.

'One began to trot towards me and so I decided to head for the gate. Imagine my surprise as one by one they all followed. I opened the 'five bar' and slowly but surely made my way well into the next field followed by every single goat. Finally, I turned gently and headed back closing the gate behind me. The expression on my colleagues' faces was one of stunned disbelief - I never told them I had previously been tipped off that their owner was a woman and they always followed her every-where.'

'How long did you work as a bailiff?' Jodi was serious now and I took a deep breath.

'Well, I came through my probation success-fully and still have the letter confirming me as London's first ever female bailiff. But the first task I was given when out on my own was to evict an elderly couple from their flatlet home over a shop. He was recovering from heart surgery and I just couldn't do it, so I simply rang up and resigned. My employers were really kind and wrote stating their regrets and even asked me to reconsider, but my mind was made up.

'The last job I had before I became totally unemployable was as a van driver. How I got it in the first place I shall never know, although I got an inkling sometime later when the manager got the sack because he failed a breathalyser.

'My first delivery was to an address in Richmond about four miles from the depot. I left at eight a.m. and rang in at eleven a.m. to say I couldn't find it. The manager told me it was on the left down the High Street, I told him it was Richmond I couldn't find.' Jodi fell about laughing yet again. 'By midday I still hadn't found it and reversing into a side road I collided with another van. The driver was none-too-pleased but I admitted liability and we exchanged names and addresses. He pointed me halfheartedly in the general direction of Richmond and off I set once again. I had travelled barely three hundred yards when I saw a man crossing the road ahead of me. I was only travelling slowly but my attention was focused mainly on the road signs. The next thing I knew he was sat on my bonnet.' Jodi's glee turned to horror. 'God!' she said for the umpteenth time. 'What happened next?'

Now, I was chuckling. 'I got out shaking like a leaf and helped him off. He said he was all right and seemed keen to get away from me as soon as possible. I got back in the van and reversed out of the way of other vehicles to let them pass and heard a muffled crunch. I got out, looked round the back and the same poor chap was on the floor in a heap. 'No! No! Get away,' he screamed, and ran off down the road. The last sight I had of him was looking over his shoulder to make sure I wasn't following.' Jodi was holding her sides. 'And that's not the end.' I said almost triumphantly. 'Five minutes later I shot a red light and hit a van who was correctly going through in his direction on green. I admitted blame and somehow got home in one piece, then rang the manager to tell him to come and pick up his van. I never did find Richmond.'

Jodi and I walked for a while after our refreshments, mainly in silence. I decided not to spoil the good humour of the afternoon by telling her of my anorexia and body mutilation.

CHAPTER SEVENTEEN

HEATHROW DIET

Peter and I were like brother and sister. We were great friends and I loved him dearly, an agape love which to date has survived a quarter of a century.

Not without a thousand terrible drunken arguments, some incredible highs and a complete and utter false interpretation from my perception, of his lack of physical interest in me. I realise now I humiliated him through an insanity created by a lifetime of abuse, further perpetuated by drink and drugs. To me, love had been fashioned by the vilest kind of abusers, who had graduated into my adult life by virtue of a sinister inveterate instinct, which led me ceaselessly into the path of those who would do me most harm. Peter was the outstanding exception. He was, and still is noble and dignified, seen by the majority who know him as one of nature's gentlemen. The fact this simple, yet beautiful persona had eluded me is a terrible indictment on the lovely Auntie Joan, huggable Billy Gruff, Paul the steward with the beautiful smile, and all the other irresistible and trusted people who formed the evil perverts of my world.

Initially, I construed Peter's reluctance to play the game the only way I knew it, as a result of the fact that it was I who was the iniquitous one, guilty of the heinous crime of corrupting everyone I came into contact with. I began to mutilate myself with ever increasing regularity, and found peace only as I watched my blood pump gently from my veins.

I intentionally spared Jodi the heavy stuff and the following day she left for home having enjoyed her short break. 'Especially the bit I spent with you,' she said as I waved her off at the station. We had arranged for me to telephone her as soon as I arrived back in London, her home in Berkshire was only a short drive from my own flat in Middlesex. I had barely known her for two days yet somehow I felt it was to be the beginning of a lasting friendship. Long after her train had departed the station I sat on the platform in the shade contemplating the heavy stuff, thinking long and hard and of awful times in my concerted effort to lay the ghosts forever.

Peter had eventually obtained work of sorts. He was still drinking of course, but his humiliation created by the ignominy of becoming tea boy during the building of terminal four at Heathrow where he had once held a senior position, was deadened by the anaesthetic that is alcohol. He went on to clean cars and then graduated somewhat into the catering trade as a waiter. The sack due to his drinking terminated some of the jobs, but a strange development began to take place. Peter started to have long periods of sobriety, some as much as six months or more and with hindsight I am convinced he already knew he and alcohol were not altogether compatible. During this time my life and general state of health was declining rapidly. An event which contributed to this in no small way, took place at my tennis club where I had become less able to play tennis, but an expert at falling off barstools. A young man whom I fancied as obsessively as everything else I took an avid interest in, remarked I was becoming podgy. I was 5' 4", 8 ½ stone (119 lbs) and wore a size 12 erring on the smaller side of it. A month later I had lost a stone. Once I had gone for two days without any food, my appetite disappeared and I was euphoric. Three months elapsed and not a morsel of solid food passed my lips, yet my alcohol intake had trebled. I was constantly in deep depression and plagued by memories of childhood sexual abuse. As the weeks passed, I became more and more committed to the theory that I was to blame. I was bad and had to be punished. The only person who knew how truly depraved I had been was me, it therefore became my responsibility to exert maximum suffering. I found pictures of myself both as a child and when I was growing up, tore them into little pieces and performed a ceremonial burning. As the flames consumed my images, I slowly and deliberately cut deeply into my arms with razor blades I kept in plentiful supply. As my life blood drained away onto a garden lawn, or stained deep red in stark contrast to the white enamel of my bath, I basked in the gratification of my agony. It was a perverse pleasure, inexplicable in its absurdity yet beautiful in its satisfaction. My alcohol intake determined how quickly I telephoned for help, twice circumstances saved my life which had echoes of Miss Lewis's religious teachings. Once I awoke with my wrist doubled up underneath my body, acting as a tourniquet from heaven. On another occasion Anne, from my chambermaid days, called unexpectedly and drove me to accident and emergency. Mostly I just sliced for an insane pleasure, enjoying the torment for my misdeeds. By the time I was thirty years of age, the skin on my arms became so thin in places because it was never given chance to heal between cutting, I could not straighten them without causing bleeding.

Years of my life are a blur. Imagine a heavy party night and the struggle to remember everything that happened when you awake the following day. Then consider drinking continually for years on end and the prolonged amnesia that results by definition of the anaesthetic effect. Some terribly embarrassing events are retained, some even amusing. Most are confined to a faculty waste bin.

One night I was invited through a friend to an upmarket fortieth dinner party celebration. I was drunk when I arrived, danced seductively with the hostesses' father who was slightly tipsy himself, and finally called a complete halt to the proceedings by mounting the rail on the landing and threatening to throw myself off into the hallway below.

I had long given up trying to find a love of my own and was not sure what I was looking for anyway. I settled for forcing myself into other people's lives and frequently beds. I recall one poor man in particular, and an event which epitomised my achievement of attaining a reputation as dumbo supreme, that occurred one winter evening close to Christmas time.

His name was Des who for reasons of his own, always left a small window open in the downstairs toilet of his house even when he was out. It was far too tiny to climb through unless you were a very small child...or anorexic! I had only eaten intermittently since being called podgy and as I now weighed in at a regular six stone (84lbs), I was sure I could get through the window. I wore the tiniest of mini skirts, and the pubs were turning out at just about the moment I became trapped, with legs kicking on the outside and muffled shouts coming from within. It must have been quite a sight and only groping hands from revellers and perverts alike provided the impetus for me to complete my passage. I climbed into his bed and as seductively as my drunken state would allow, awaited his return. And waited, and waited...and passed out.

The following morning I was awakened by the telephone ringing. I hoped it would stop but it did not and I struggled from the bed falling onto the floor on my knees, then on one knee and painfully into standing position. Finally I lifted the receiver.

'Nikki, Nikki is that you?' My voice sounded a long way away and was barely a whisper as I answered. 'Des, where have you been?'

'Oh! For God's sake Nikki, I saw your public performance last night as I drove up and fortunately managed to drive on without you seeing me. I spent half the night trying to find a place to kip.'

I replaced the receiver, splashed some water on my face and left through the front door shutting it firmly behind me. All I could think of was the alluring charm I thought I possessed when I had been drinking obviously only existed in my imagination, and it certainly deserted me when the glass was empty. It was also further confirmation of what I had come to believe as I had grown into adulthood - I was an odious despicable and corrupt woman.

Just before Christmas Samantha, who liked Peter even less than he liked her, persuaded me to evict him from the house. In a drunken temper, with blood pouring from razor cuts on my arms, I threw him out onto the street on Christmas Eve. He even turned and smiled apologetically as he walked away, clasping one suitcase containing all his possessions. My action was made even more unjust by the fact that six months previously both Peter's parents had died within weeks of one another, and he had given me half his legacy - ten thousand pounds in cash.

* * * * * * * * * * *

In the months that followed, and mainly
because I felt a responsibility for Samantha, I cut
down on my alcohol intake and began to drink
milk, eat yoghurt and soup, usually Heinz tomato.
I managed to secure a part-time job at W.H.Smith
and for a while I kept myself together. I still muti-
lated my arms and legs, but superficially and
mainly in private though Samantha did call an
ambulance on at least one occasion. Slowly but
surely I slipped back into my old degenerative life
pattern, too much alcohol, too little food and several half-hearted suicide attempts. Unexpectedly
W.H.Smith generously came to my rescue and
sent me to a convalescent home at their expense in
West Sussex. It was a stopping place, offering temporary respite along the way. In a relatively short
time, my life took the shape of an inebriate
woman, wandering from one pathetic single-
roomed bedsit to another, encompassing relationships as incomprehensible and vague as ships
passing in the night. My drunken binges escalated
into a terrible violence. Not against my fellow man,
but aimed at destroying possessions and everything around me varying from those that belonged
to me to those which did not. The reaction of the
property owners was one of stunned disbelief and
rapid eviction.

I trudged the streets and knew little of the
day and even less of the night. One early morning
I awoke in yet another bus shelter cramped, cold

and ill. It was at this point the divine hand led me to my friend Jacqui at the David Lloyd Tennis Club. She asked questions, I answered as best I could but nothing made sense. Incredibly my luck changed, she offered a temporary bed in a house she shared.

Jacqui had many wealthy clients at the club who saw her professionally for massage, pedicure, manicure, body waxing and reflexology. That afternoon while I slept in her private room, I was on her mind a lot. She talked to one of her clients, a wealthy woman from Chiswick in West London, and because of me discussed alcoholism and anorexia at length. The woman talked about a man she knew who had become a tramp due to years of alcohol abuse and now ran day centres to help others because he had found a way back to sanity. He had helped one of her relatives turn his life around; his name was Justin and for me an incredible miracle was about to take place.

There was a long complicated procedure, and my drinking certainly did not stop immediately, but effectively my recovery began the following morning and continues to this day. Addictions and compulsive disorders take a lifetime to enter into. If the victim wants to be as good at being sober, for example learning to be unobsessive and proficient at doing things most people take for granted, it takes at least a similar amount of time and effort to that which they put into their drinking. Justin told me I had to unlearn all the bad habits I had been training myself into for years. He said a big

149

part of me had to undergo a kind of death.

When alcohol was eventually removed from my life we revealed all the reasons why I drank to excess in the first place. The task of putting me back together was just that. Justin had to disassemble my irrationality and put the pieces back together in the right order, a metamorphosis that was terrifying to experience. The effect on him was no less traumatic. One day I shall never forget was the culmination of a three week period when I had lapsed into complete madness. He snapped. Picked me up like a rag doll and recoiled his arm to smash a mighty fist into my head, which was trapped against the wall of his office. His face was soaked in sweat - time stood still - I could barely breathe and just felt a slight tremble in his grip. Slowly he let me down into a heap on the floor where I lay gasping for breath. He opened a cupboard in the corner, took out a bottle of wine and a pack of razor blades and smashed them down on the office table. The wine was of the screw top type, and grabbing a glass from a water tray he filled it with wine and took a blade out of its protective wrap.

'Right! drink the shit you ungrateful bitch. Cut your fucking arms at my expense. And yes you are a fat, ugly bastard just as you always suspected you were. Do it!' he roared.

I did not look up. My tears splashed onto the vinyl tiled floor making puddles and I knew perhaps through instinct, despite my misery, something had changed forever.

It was definitely not instantaneous. The concentration of the symptoms of my diagnosed anorexia, bulimia, alcoholism and substance misuse shifted inexorably from one condition to the other, making them harder to deal with due to withdrawal, and the root of my urges moving from one to the other uncontrollably. I began eating under Justin's watchful eye almost afraid not to in case he withdrew his succour. Anorexia became bulimia. I was anxious to impress, desperate to show the extent of my commitment by displaying co-operation. At the first opportunity, I would escape to vomit. Just as I thought I had done so successfully, there came a knock on a lavatory door or his head would appear around a bush in a garden. He would say nothing, there was no need, his expression was a mixture of pity tinged with contempt. One day he told me the contempt was because he had seventy people on his list awaiting help and he could not move on to them until I decided to respond. I told him to move on, perhaps I wasn't worth it. He said he could have saved two people with the time he had already spent on me. I sobbed in despair. Then he spoke words I shall remember forever.

'You are fighting a battle you cannot win. Why don't you surrender and rejoin the human race, then you can help me save lives?'

My recollections of the period are sketchy, but with the benefit of hindsight I am convinced I was born again that day.

CHAPTER EIGHTEEN

THE LADY IN THE LAKE

Suddenly I realised the sun had gone down, I was cold and the railway station an extremely draughty place to sit. As I got up from where I had been sitting, cramp in my legs made me catch my breath and looking at my watch I became aware Jodi was long gone.

I was more than grateful when I arrived back in my room at the hotel. I half undressed, put on my dressing gown and dozed off peacefully on the comfy bed I had become quite accustomed to. I dreamed wonderful dreams of all the people I had helped with problems like mine. Many had gone on to live normal, happy and often very successful lives. We were all together in a wondrous place laughing, joking and enjoying a magnificent feast and drinking colourful juices and non-alcoholic punch.

I awoke slowly and gently, barely an hour had passed, I lay quietly and peacefully basking in the joy of others and the sheer elation of knowing I had been privileged to play a small part in their recoveries. Inexplicably, although grateful for the individual attention I had received from Justin, I envied the camaraderie that had developed once the residential Chaucer Clinic replaced his day centres. I had sampled a short stay of sorts, but it was not quite the same as the programme I was now administering to others as General Manager. John, for example had been sleeping in a local park and he now had a business, wife and child. Susanne's husband had taken her back in sobriety and a child was born - I wondered if she would have recovered had Jacqui not helped me. Bill, Tony, Kenny, Lynn ... so many, I felt guilty I could not remember all their names. Some, I shall never forget.

Albert Johannson was the first black player to appear in an FA Cup Final at Wembley. He played for Leeds United F.C against Liverpool in the 1965 extra time epic.

On the 16th June 1992 Albert was a million miles away from the glamour of major league football and adoring fans. He shook uncontrollably, his face and hair were soaked in sweat, the air smelled of stale alcohol and he vomited involuntarily into a white plastic bucket I kept especially for times like this.

'I used to play in white for Leeds.' Albert, eyes red and streaming managed a smile through the irony as he pointed at the bucket.

'Please be kind to me.' His voice tailed off into a whisper. I swallowed hard.

Daily Sun sports journalist John Sadler had

been caring enough to make the referral. I cannot recall the precise details just a phone call from an agent who I soon sussed wanted a fit Albert so he could get a big percentage of something in the future. Sadler would have been furious had he known this man had spirited Albert away before treatment was complete because the chance of a fast buck suddenly presented itself.

Nevertheless, Albert stayed in my care for three months of a scheduled eight month programme before this happened. We shared many confidences all of which will remain so, however, certain things he would have been pleased for me to share. He had an extremely high regard for Leeds United and later England manager Don Revie, although one story made for sober listening. 'We all took a small glass of whisky from a tray and knocked it back before we ran onto the pitch.' He told me this as he mixed cement during his work therapy programme, I remember him smiling ruefully his eyes looking away from mine.

He loved his granddaughter Samantha dearly, although he had not seen her and never went anywhere without her photograph. His favourite story though, concerned his initial arrival in the UK.

'All us kids in South Africa believed that everyone who lived in the U.K was staggeringly rich by definition,' he smiled one eye slightly but endearingly out of alignment. 'We played football every hour of every day at home and as soon as I arrived it continued that way with one big difference. I was given more money than I could have imagined in my wildest dreams and everything but everything was done for me. Car of my choice, feted everywhere I went, I rarely bought a drink...!

'I wrote home and told my friends and one in particular managed to get to Britain. When he arrived at Heathrow he simply said he was a friend of Albert's and demanded a car and an immediate supply of cash.'

Albert laughed heartily everytime he told the story, but always without fail when the mirth subsided, he became serious and added that it was not really funny.

He was born in Johannesburg on the 13th March 1940 although for some strange reason insisted for his medical records it was the 12th March 1942. Football records show he made his debut against Swansea Town, although Albert preferred it to be against Aston Villa at Villa Park where he scored the only goal in a 0-1 win. The record book is probably correct, half confirmed by a glint in Albert's eye. His version was probably inspired by Justin's devotion to the Villa.

He talked lovingly of Germiston Coloured School and Germiston Colliers where he is still remembered in the highest esteem. When his professional career ended he returned to South Africa and coached a Germiston side, but eventually returned to England forever hoping his luck would change.

I pointed out he would determine his own future if he continued to abuse alcohol.

'But when I start I can't stop,' he would say. 'Simple then,' I would reply. 'Don't start....' Albert almost believed me.

From his death defying arrival for treatment, when consultant psychiatrist Dr. David Marjot fed him Chlordiazepoxide like Smarties until he stopped shaking, he eventually progressed to kicking a ball with the other patients in the Chaucer football team.

Those near to him, inspired mainly by gain, must have been impressed - sadly, chronically sick alcoholics suddenly appearing miraculously cured, is a major misconception responsible for the death of thousands. We at Chaucer Clinic call it the 'infamous red herring'.

He was persuaded to attend a dinner in his honour and was spun an unforgivable untruth by a devious man who assured Albert I had said he could have a glass of celebration champagne as a one-off. He was also told he would not get a testimonial match if he did not attend - another lie, Leeds United had never committed themselves to a testimonial football match for Albert Johannson. Three days later having failed to return for treatment he was found drunk in a Leeds gutter. On 29th September 1995 he was found dead in a high-rise slum flat. He had been dead for several days.

Gillian was a patient whose story had a happier ending, though her progress was beset by the worst kind of tragedy.

She was forty years old when she took her

first drink and was hooked from day one. Within two years of the first fateful mouthful she was admitted to the Gordon Hospital, Westminster, eighteen months later she came to me.

Gillian worked incredibly hard for her sobriety and just as her future seemed secure her newly born granddaughter Kylie, died from septicemia. The whole family were devastated - Gillian was inconsolable.

Out of adversity emerged veritable courage. She rose above her illness, held her family and sobriety firm, and inspired a deep agape love to pull her progenies back from the brink with a resilience even Gillian was unaware she possessed.

A black cloud suddenly descended to mar this happy memory. There were some who could not be helped and went on to live a life of torment. Others died an agonising death, and one even created a national media mystery which remains unsolved to this day. She, was the lady in the lake.

The moment I first saw her I was struck by her gentle beauty, on the other hand she had a disquieting amorphous which gave her a phantom-like appearance. She was painfully thin, had many razor scars on her arms like mine, and spoke of love and peace without conviction. She was accompanied by a nurse from Whipps Cross Hospital where she had been treated for body mutilation and addiction. I was introduced, she moved towards me unsteadily and gave me an enormously affectionate hug which seemed to last forever. I was anxious not to prise myself free for fear of creating an impression of rejection, but felt a slight relief when she let me go. I noticed her midriff was bared conducive with fashion. Two words were tattooed one above and one below her navel - Funky Pumpkin.

I led her gently to the interview room and began filling in the mandatory assessment form. It proved extremely difficult. Her powers of concentration had diminished alarmingly, the explanation for which became clearer as she described her addiction to alcohol and drugs, particularly cocaine. She was extremely proud of her mother whom she described as a nurse and expressed devotion for her little sister who was eight years of age. The meeting was punctuated with pauses after each question, which gave the impression she had either not heard, or not understood. Once I repeated myself. It was when I asked her full name and date of birth.

'I heard you the first time.' Her words were firm but softly spoken. 'My name is Carol McKewen but you can call me Maxi.'

'As you would,' I said. I'd had a hard day, it was going to be an even longer night, but I regretted my attempt at humourous sarcasm immediately and said so. She did not reply. I ploughed on. 'Occupation?' I spoke slowly now. I had seen busy-bee Andre Agassi slowed down by the unique artistry of Pete Sampras during a frenetic game of tennis with sheer professional manipulation. I guessed this was Carol's game plan and she was good at it, I wanted to be better.

'I'm a prostitute, but I choose my clients very carefully and only ever go out with men who really need to be loved.' The words remained calm, delivered softly and matter of fact but with a subtle change, her eyes never left mine.

I studied her momentarily. She had long blonde hair which was obviously natural, it contained a degree of red pigmentation which gave it a slight sandy appearance. Her skin was very pale, of the difficult to tan variety and her face was freckled exquisitely, made so by its shape and the softness of her eyes.

'Why do you like to be called Maxi?' I asked not expecting a logical answer and putting the assessment form to one side. She was taking her time again and I decided the form filling could wait for another day at least. Her hands were beginning to tremble slightly and I calculated she was in the very early stages of withdrawing from the alcohol I could smell on her breath.

'My little sister is called Maxine. If I share her name perhaps God will allow some of the bad things intended for her, to happen to me instead.' I discarded my pen as well as the form.

'Tell me about your childhood.' She sat back deeply into a luxurious settee I had taken from Justin's office when he wasn't looking, and prepared myself for someone else's hell. I needn't have bothered, she was in no mood to unload. She did say it had been horrific, intimated she had been abused by an alcoholic father who had taken a drug overdose and died, but refused to say if it had been mental, physical or sexual.

The next eleven days were feverish, frenzied and furious. She was admitted on a Thursday and we rushed her to accident and emergency four times before Saturday lunchtime. She slashed her wrist in front of other patients with blades which appeared like magic. We had searched her belongings upon admission and found nothing - not that there was much to search, but no matter how hard we looked, we could not discover her supply. With echoes of the past, I found a beautiful wooden box in the clinic woodwork department and placed in it six small hygienically packed bandages, a quantity of lint and a pack of razor blades, then called her to my office.

'Here you are Maxi, here's a supply of your favourite things. Use them whenever you wish and kindly bandage yourself, because we can't spare the time to keep going backwards and forwards to the hospital.' She paused only for a moment, took the box and turned tail - no further mutilation took place during her stay.

Maxi still posed a few problems. She was extremely difficult to place for work therapy, finally I put her to work in the garden and sent her to her room to put on some working clothes - she returned in crotchless leather trousers and a bra with holes designed to expose her nipples; of course they were the tools of her trade!

She did try hard for a day or so, but poor Maxi was not of this world. Alcohol and drugs had inflicted serious psychological damage and she floated in and out of reality in a most disturbing manner. Such was the damage inflicted, predominately in her early teens, everything that gave her pleasure had a sexual connotation. Everyone with whom she came into contact was shown her gold ringed pierced nipple and rubber nurses outfit, together with school uniform and other bits and pieces all of which featured among her meagre possessions. I made several attempts to get through to her, journeying into a world of closed doors and mystical intelligence, sadly I was too late. Maxi decided sobriety could not offer the fun and excitement alcohol and drugs provided, and one evening I received a telephone call to say she had discharged herself. Her parting words were along the lines that she had problems in her private life only drink could suppress. I did not believe her - all addicts spoke that way - I had no way of knowing her mother and young eight year old sister had been brutally raped sometime previously, and the perpetrator's trial was currently in progress at the Old Bailey.

Four months later I was stood in a queue at my favourite newsagents in Uxbridge, when a headline in a newspaper caught my attention.

'Mystery of the lady in the lake'

The article described the body of a young woman found floating in an ornamental pond in the Italian Gardens at Lancaster Gate in Kensington. It went

161

on to say the police were treating the death as suspicious, although there were no signs of violence on her body and a post mortem had proved inconclusive. She remained unidentified despite being described as distinctive with long strawberry blonde hair. On her tummy two words were tattooed - Funky Pumpkin...

I recalled during one of our talks a lovely story she told of walking in the Italian Gardens in Kensington with the boy she hoped to marry. 'We made beautiful plans for the future,' she had said. 'I always go there when I need to be happy.'

At the inquest the coroner returned an open verdict... Maxi's journey had ended where she had hoped her future would begin.

CHAPTER NINETEEN

ODYSSEY THROUGH SPACE, TIME AND INSANITY

Thinking of Maxi brought to the forefront of my mind my hell revisited, which had proved to be a resurgence of experiences old and new. An opportunity to reflect and reconsider the bizarre, perverse, enigmatic and utterly outrageous. Yet somehow I had evaded the most vital issue of all. How I had dealt with the terror, anguish and misery of my journey back to something resembling a recovery. Like the worn-out family car, which had undergone one too many visits to the garage repairers, my body had been ready for the scrapyard. I had reached Justin on the equivalent of a breakdown truck, and he had eyed me in much the same way as a car-breaker scrutinizes a wreck. I was now forcing myself to think deeply of the worst of my hell and how I had returned from it. It had to be done, which was why I was here. I racked my brains!

Meeting Justin had not been straightforward. I arrived as just another patient, he accepted me as such, it was not to be that way, because although destined to be an extremely rocky road...I came to stay. I recall being timid, fearful and so frail I barely had the strength to stand. I find it hard to concede now but I would have obeyed any instruction given to me however irrelevant, silly or perverted. I had been programmed by life to do as bid whatever the cost no matter the pain, and humiliation was not a word in my vocabulary. It was indeed lucky for me that fate for once, had delivered me into safe hands.

Although Justin's work operated from day centres, they were short leases and as a result he was always on the move. His most recent acquisition however, was promising to be more permanent and was in a disused ward on a hospital estate in west London. Despite this, I had been referred to his home which to all intents and purposes seemed to be where most of his activities helping addicts was run from, it was a simple terrace house but there were beds everywhere. I was glad I still had one with Jacqui Whitaker even if it was hanging from a thread, at least there I could have my secret tipple.

Protocol insisted my G.P. give me a referral in the form of a sealed letter for Justin which I handed to him. He read the words and still looking at the sheet of paper, sank back into a club chair with an expression on his face that one would normally associate with reaction to an unexpected Inland Revenue demand.

'I suppose you're aware all is not well in your

world?' I remember not responding immediately because my brain refused to concentrate, so he went on talking slowly and deliberately.

'I trust your doctor has informed you fully regarding the extent of your mental and physical condition?' I nodded. He looked deeply into my eyes and beyond and I suddenly realized I had continued to nod and rock backwards and forwards in my seat just as I always had during times of stress since my childhood.

His voice began to drone and then fade into the deepest recesses of my mind as my ability to concentrate deteriorated even further, and an indeterminable period of time passed by. I could hear conversation mixed and muffled, voices merging into one another and occasionally I picked out my name. Then I was back at Jacqui's.

Justin called on me regularly at my temporary home during the weeks that followed, always by appointment but of course a constant threat to my now secret drinking. Although not altogether sure why, I was afraid of him and his ideology of permanent abstinence by way of a cure for all the problems in my life. Somehow the fear provided a discipline that, for a short time, prevented me getting smashed. I tippled regularly, yet to my relief even Jacqui was delighted because my alcohol intake was no longer sufficient to provoke a personality change.

One day Justin arrived for one of my therapy sessions, during which he usually gave an hour to offering me advice and listened to all my problems. On this occasion without even bothering to sit down he said: 'I won't be coming again, at least not for the time being, call me if you want to stop drinking!' He'd gone before I had a chance to react. I told Jacqui when she returned my treatment had ended, and I was now free to have a glass of wine...or two! That night I gatecrashed a party, wrecked a stranger's front room and returned to destroy the accommodation kindly afforded rent free by my only friend. I came to twenty four hours later. It was eleven o'clock at night and there was congealed blood all over my body, my worldly possessions, and even more of Jacqui's smashed beyond repair, and hardly a pane of glass intact in the modern windows. Her curtains were ripped to shreds, together with bed linen and most of my clothes. Two of the wooden panels in the door had gaping holes a small dog could walk through, and the bed was good only for a skip. I looked around in disbelief, and cried like a baby.

I tried to stand but the pain was too great, and it took a full quarter of an hour to crawl the ten feet to the telephone which was situated in the hallway. Justin answered and I begged him to come and save me.

'Can't come at the moment, it's late and I'm reading the paper'. A silence ensued, I was not so brain dead I couldn't work out I was of less importance than a tabloid newspaper. I already knew I was worthless, I was just not brave enough to end my own life, save myself further pain and spare those around me from a millstone they had done nothing to deserve.

'Are you still there?' Justin sounded only vaguely interested. 'Yes, but I wish I was dead, I really wish I was dead.' My voice died without the rest of me and there was a further silence. 'Gonna rain tomorrow according to the forecast.' I heard the rustle as he turned the page of his newspaper. 'And Aston Villa have signed a new goalscorer from Liverpool.' Justin exaggerated his Birmingham accent intentionally, and then with a perfect copy of my own West Country dialect. 'I s'pose u think oi'm gooin to cum runnin' to 'elp?'

I had completely capitulated. I'd heard of rock bottoms, this was as low as I ever wanted to go and I told him so. 'You get one last chance' was all he said before I heard the click in my ear that ended our conversation. The unfathomable enigma that is addiction had its final say. I was aware a can still held half a glass of lager left at the moment I had passed into unconsciousness the night before. I poured it with trembling hands but drank it quickly. It was 11.50pm on the 22nd September 1989. I had no way of knowing, but I had just had my last alcoholic drink.

He arrived in less than half an hour, I hadn't moved an inch, he lifted me bodily and put me on the back seat of a large luxury car. I told him all I had to bring was in a bin bag which he would find amongst the debris, he returned in a matter of seconds and we drove away. Mercifully, I lost consciousness and met monsters beyond the imaginings of normal folk - they abused me in medieval fashion and I willingly accepted the torture I knew I richly deserved.

Suddenly it was daylight. I lay in a single bed alone, it was the first thing I checked. I was glad, my head ached and my body too, literally everywhere. Vaguely I recognized my surroundings as Justin's house and his delightful wife Penny arrived with a cup of tea, a cheerful smile and the bubbly personality I hated her for. I stayed for a few days and than a friend of Penny's offered me a temporary bed providing I didn't drink, I agreed. The other condition was I went out with Justin everyday visiting alcoholics. 'People like you and me.' He had said. I was getting stronger but I had no resistance against fact - I couldn't drink alcohol and function normally this was for sure, an undisputed reality to which I readily agreed.

Justin had many calls to make, so every morning I washed and dressed in haste. He talked incessantly as we drove from place to place about alcohol addiction, pill popping and smoking pot. He told me a story about some stupid bloody Russian neurologist who got so drunk he realized alcohol had caused him brain damage. Then on second thoughts it might have been that the Russian discovered the condition in somebody else or some such nonsense! Anyway, they named it after him. Then I went to sleep and woke each time the car engine stopped. He would utter pleasantries and make a house call, then the next stop would be at a cafe for a cup of tea and cakes. I ate everything he gave me and then threw it up in the loo so he wouldn't know. When we got back to the car the bastard gave me a bottle of water and told me to wash my mouth out in case the vomit mixed with stomach acids rotted my teeth. I think it was day three when my head stopped aching.

At the end of each day we returned to his home where Penny had prepared a dinner for us. On the first occasion I was given a great big plate with about one tablespoonful of food in the middle of it. It looked a bit like an island in the middle of an ocean. 'Not so much to sick-up!' Justin said without as much as a glance up from his enormous meal. His wife was solemn - I thought I saw a tear - I knew she liked me, I hated her, she had Justin and I wanted him to myself because he was the only man in the whole world I had ever met I could trust. Each night I was dropped off at my temporary digs.

As if Penny wasn't enough, he had Martine. A smarmy super-efficient secretary who had worked for him forever, and I wanted her dead!

I shook my head violently, suddenly realizing I had been thinking of my alcoholic insanity so intensely I was inadvertently slipping back into a psychotic lunacy, and I shuddered at the thought of the silky thread that so terrifyingly represented the divide between sanity and total madness. I was forcing myself to recall those terrible days when I went through the worst of my recovery as part of my journey of re-invention. Only someone with similar experiences would understand the necessity and the reasons why.

Paranoia was my Mrs. Hyde and easily came to mind. I was convinced all manner of elaborate conspiracies were being plotted against me. If I walked into a room and a conversation between two people within stopped abruptly, I knew for sure a secret plot of monumental proportions was afoot.

Over a relatively short period of a month or so, Justin moved all of his business and addiction activities to the hospital building he now called 'Chaucer Clinic', and opened it as a day centre and sort of head office. I remember very little all things considered, except I did most of the cleaning and there was plenty of it. Gradually, between what I now see with hindsight as tantrums, he gave me additional jobs which I did, and somehow still managed to lose myself amongst the dozens of non-drinking drunks who wandered around doing various tasks, in what he now called a rehab. Tins of paint and building materials old and new mysteriously appeared, and to me anyway, mysteriously disappeared into the structure of the building, filling up holes in the roof and brightening the appearance of just about everything. Furniture and beds, bric-a-brac and most of what could be found in an average hotel materialised out of thin air and through it all, the stupid Penny and infuriating Martine goody-bloody-two-shoes kept up a charade of forcing themselves to say nice things to me, buying me presents I had to accept for fear of offending my beloved Justin, and even pretending to worry about whether I ate or not.

One day, about six weeks after my last alcoholic drink but six thousandth planned piss-up that had failed to materialise, Justin in his wisdom, or more likely madness as far as I was concerned, decided it would become my job to answer the office telephone. Some hope - I hid in a cupboard and locked it from the inside. The coaxing continued for a while then everything went quiet. Time dragged, I cannot say for how long, but I could not give in, after all there was a principle at stake. Trouble was after a while I couldn't remember what the principle was, so I thought I would let myself out. The lock opened easily enough but something was blocking the front of the cupboard. The doors opened just enough for me to see that someone had dragged a heavy desk across so I couldn't get out even if I wanted to. I went berserk, or at least as frenzied as you can get when restricted to barely six inches of movement. I shouted, screamed, threatened and all to no avail, then Justin's voice sounded after what seemed an eternity: "Well, will you answer the phone for me Nikki?" "No you fuckin' arsehole, I'll see you dead before I answer your fuckin' phone!" "Bye for now then." The footsteps got fainter.

"Good afternoon, Chaucer Clinic." It was three hours later and I was sure the caller would still be able to hear the tears in my voice. "Oh! Sorry, I must have the wrong number," said a voice at the other end of the line. The phone went dead. Genuine applause rang out from Justin, I knew he meant it, he would never deceive me. I smiled - inside and out. That night, just for once, it was with a good feeling that I went back to my digs.

Five or six very confused weeks later he introduced me to a friend and business associate of his, one David Ellis, who desperately needed a female voice to answer the phone at his garage.

"All you have to do is take messages and not only will it give you confidence, it will be a change of scenery." Justin gave me a warm hug and I knew he must be right, and no matter what, I wanted to get better.

Sleep eluded me that night and by 4a.m. I knew for sure Justin, just like everyone else before him, wanted me out of his life. I didn't go to Mr. Ellis's, I walked around the local shopping centre instead. After two hours I plucked up the courage to telephone him from a call-box. He was very forgiving, said he understood and told me to get in touch with Justin at once. I could hardly believe my luck - his reaction was exactly the same and the kindly Mr. Ellis picked me up and drove me back to Chaucer Clinic.

On my first day back, I took a telephone call I was truly delighted to receive. My ex-husband Peter de Villiers, with whom I had kept in touch somewhat hypocritically given the acrimonious way in which we parted, had tracked me down and was calling to enquire about my health. He had apparently met up with Dr. Webb my GP, who had predictably painted a none-too-pretty picture of my current condition, and managed to track me down to Chaucer. Peter was living in a bedsit in Middlesex and had been sober two years, saving all his money from his menial jobs in order to pay the fare back to his beloved South Africa. He was due to go any day and amongst other things, asked me if I would like to take over his humble home. Justin who had to be consulted, took an instant liking to Peter, and was in full agreement.

One thing did bother my mentor, and that was me living alone, even allowing for the fact it was now three months since I had drunk alcohol. And although I now had a purpose in life at the clinic it was a fragile peace and lacking in harmony to the extreme; alcohol was responsible for enormous damage.

Martine, Penny, Peter and Justin helped me move and subtly change the appearance of Peter's home to one more appropriate for a female. It was a surprisingly long job but finally they were gone and I was left sober, drug free and alone with my demons. Alcohol had deadened the pain. What I now faced in solitary confinement was the humiliation and knowledge my life was not only in ruins, but in the quietness of this tiny place I had nothing to anaesthetise the pain or dull the madness in my brain. I found a blade, cut my wrist and bled in pleasure, relief and finally unconsciousness.

I awoke several hours later back at the clinic with Justin holding my hand. 'Good job I had a key,' he said quietly without elaboration. I did not answer, there was nothing to say.

'Do you like animals?' It had been several

173

minutes since either of us had spoken and at first his words did not register. 'Yes I love animals,' I eventually answered falteringly.

'Good,' he said. 'Because I've got a little friend for you to look after.' He picked up a telephone, dialled a number on the internal system and spoke a brief sentence into the receiver.

Two minutes later there was a knock on the door and the dreaded Martine, looking somewhat different and holding a beautiful puppy in her arms, walked into the room.

'It's a Cavalier Spaniel, his name's Charlie and he's a present from Justin'. She said with genuine warmth. I looked spellbound.

Two of the most beautiful days of my adult life later, a friend drove me to the vets to have my first ever puppy inoculated.

The vet was a lovely man who had seen cats of mine in the past, and we were having a most pleasant chat as he put Charlie through various tests. Suddenly, his face took on a serious expression and he stood back, "I'm sorry Nikki, the little darling has an extremely serious heart murmur, I doubt he'll live more than a few weeks."

Crashing noises sounded in my head. Flashing colours filled my vision and I grabbed my baby from him and ran blindly away from this sudden threat of death. I could feel the breath on my neck of hordes of chasing hippies, car horns blaring out and finally the impact of my body on tarmac.

It was two days before I regained consciousness back in the security of Chaucer Clinic. Later I discovered I'd had a narrow escape because a motorist had braked in time. Justin had called a friend, a consultant psychiatrist who had given me a sedative, and Justin, Penny and Martine had taken turns to keep watch. I was horrified some time later when Martine suggested I should have another dog, she said that I had been desperately unlucky and it was unlikely to ever happen again. Penny had agreed with her - I didn't hate them now, but I couldn't face a repeat of the horror.

Justin had agreed with the girls, and unbeknown to me had located another Cavalier Spaniel which he brought around to the bedsit on my first night back. I was still on medication and I don't know who was the most bewildered, me or the dog. I was still unable to grasp the events of the past few days and nights and I must have gone to sleep immediately. Daylight woke me with sun streaming through the window and a warm furry lump on my head. I lay there for a while, then abruptly it moved and a warm, wet liquid ran down my head, face and neck. It was the puppy having a pee.

I wracked my brains for a memory of where the creature could have come from. Then the phone rang and Justin's voice, music to my ears, spoke gently. "How's the little one?"

"I'm not calling it Charlie!" I screamed defiantly down the phone to Justin in a feeble attempt to make some sort of stand against I know not what. "Just as well," he said. "She's a girl!"

Like most things in my life, including friendships it was a shaky start, but a very solid and important bond soon developed. Charlotte was a lifeline - a source of unconditional love, of total trust, of unending comfort and happiness, an individual and personal being who was mine and mine alone. Others were allowed surrogate rights, but I left little doubt as to whom she belonged. Charlotte was a very important milestone in my recovery - and first to really love me.

My wristwatch alarm reminded me where I was and the fact it was time for dinner in the hotel restaurant. I thought of spaniels as I allowed the power shower to wash away the misery of my necessary journey back through space and time.

Charlie was taken back to the breeder where he died on Christmas Day while playing with his brothers and sisters.

CHAPTER TWENTY

DUDU PUKWANA - THE ORIGINAL HUGGY BEAR

The hotel reception had a small corner where places of interest and centres of entertainment were listed, some with colourful posters others by attractive handouts. One in particular caught my eye. It described a jazz night at a local hotel featuring one of the country's leading alto saxophonists. An enormous lump began to form in my throat as I remembered Dudu Pukwana who had been in recovery with me more than a decade previously in the first year of Chaucer Clinic - he had been revered in music circles the world over as the most emotive and exciting of all South African jazz musicians, and was once described by a critic as the Johnny Hodges to McGregor's Ellington. (John Fordham, The Guardian).

I sat through many hours of mutual suffering with Dudu in my very early days of sobriety when I had spent a short residential stay at Chaucer Clinic. We had cried together, trembled and hallucinated, held comforting hands while his lovely Swiss wife Barbara spoke tactful words of encouragement, and I paid special attention to his life story and was so grateful he listened patiently to mine. He was such a loveable man in a roguish sort of way, and I heard from friends and fans alike that his antics were legendary. He had only been at the clinic for a week when he knocked my door gently at eight o'clock one evening and in whispered tones told me he was going to perform with his band at a booking in Hammersmith. I was aghast. Quaking in my shoes at the thought of Justin's wrath, I pleaded with him to put his recovery first; Dudu was already halfway out of the window, saxophone first.

An enormous crash and the sound of breaking glass woke me up with a start; a clock on the wall told me it was four a.m. I became aware of huffing and puffing and the sound of another patient's voice, cautiously I followed his footsteps. The sight that met our eyes was one of devastation. An alto saxophone which had played a thousand venues lay detached from its case on the stony floor, and broken glass lay everywhere around the comatose shape of Dudu, who on his return had somehow fallen in through the window. We cleaned up the mess between us and put him to bed.

The following morning I awoke to the sound of singing and the smell of frying bacon and eggs. I dragged on my dressing gown and struggled to the kitchen where I received a raucous welcome from Dudu who looked as fresh as a daisy.

'NIKKI, NIKKI, NIKKI, sit down for break-fast.' Dudu gave me a mammoth hug as he did with everyone he cared for, and I was almost physically plonked into a seat.

'I have some money due today,' he announced emphatically. 'Mr. Justin can call and get it for me and half goes to the clinic.' With that he sat down to a massive plate of bacon, eggs, beans, mushrooms and fried bread.

'You ask Mr. Justin, here is the number.' He pushed a piece of paper to me containing a name and telephone number.

I told Justin when he arrived that the money was obviously outstanding from a long ago performance and would he plead on Dudu's behalf. Justin had been in the entertainment industry for many years, his earnings having financed his work with addicts in the early days, and I knew he would rise to the occasion. Dudu was called to the office and Justin adopted his most officious tone.

'I am calling on behalf of my client Mr. Dudu Pukwana, to whom you owe the sum of one thousand pounds from an engagement he performed on...' his voice tailed off and his attention switched to Dudu who was now sat in stony faced indignation, directed at the liberty taken by the man at the other end of the phone.

'When was this booking Dudu?' Justin's voice became only slightly friendly. Dudu answered immediately. 'Last night.' Justin's face was a picture. It changed colour at least twice, and suddenly realisation dawned on the hapless Dudu who slowly got to his feet and was out of the door before the explosion. Gripping the table with ever whitening knuckles, Justin finished the conversation and replaced the receiver. I was unsure whether to stay or go.

'Mr. Pukwana,' hissed Justin, 'was paid in advance of last nights performance and spent the lot during the course of the evening and early morning in the artistes bar. The manager even had to loan him the taxi fare to his home in Southall.' I slipped quietly away and advised Dudu to stay out of sight for an hour or two.

The following day Justin sneezed involuntarily and damaged his neck leaving him writhing in agony. Dudu, Barbara and I drove him at snails pace to the accident and emergency department at Ealing Hospital, and he spent a fortnight on Dihydrocodeine (DF118 Forte) and in a neckbrace. My everlasting memory of Dudu, which is also a tribute to this kind and beautiful man, was of him sitting together with the lovely Barbara and I, hour after hour, awaiting Justin's diagnosis. When dear Dudu died on June twenty-ninth 1990 aged fifty-two the world lost, not just a truly great musician, but a wonderful character and gentleman - a breed God makes far too few of.

Although I was a lover of jazz, I couldn't bear the prospect of watching a pretender to Dudu's alto sax throne at a local hotel no matter how good he was, so I replaced the handout and decided to retire early.

CHAPTER TWENTY-ONE

HELL AT THE VICARAGE

I switched on the television. It was the first time I had done so since booking into the hotel. The news was on and I moved to change the channel. I hated the news and news programmes as there was hardly ever any good news and I found it profoundly depressing. The item showing however, struck a chord and made me pause and watch. A young woman I had seen before, Jill Saward, had agreed to meet one of the men who had been involved in her rape some years previously. I was fascinated. Jill Saward, the victim of the Ealing Vicarage rape, was just twenty-one and a virgin when she was raped and buggered by two of the three men who broke into the vicarage where she lived with her father the Revd. Michael Saward, Vicar of St. Mary's in Ealing, west London.

The assaults upon both her boyfriend and father were vicious to the extreme, and her own ordeal unimaginable... although not to me. She was forced into oral sex by alcohol and drug crazed perpetrators carrying knives. The penis down her throat made her retch and when she did so he turned her onto her stomach and told her he was, 'going up the back as well.' He then buggered her, causing indescribable pain and penetrated her with the knife handle.

At the time the crime occurred I had read the newspaper articles and watched television coverage with the same horror as everyone else, and because of my experiences felt I wanted to write to her and tell her there was... 'life after'. I must have written at least a dozen letters - somehow I could not put my feelings into words - they all ended in the bin.

Mention of the Ealing Vicarage rape, immediately triggered memories of a particular Monday morning at work some years after the event, which had begun normally enough, but by lunchtime was developing into secret service work. The mystery started around eleven a.m. with a telephone call from a lawyer based in Staines, Middlesex. He was enquiring if our alcohol recovery project accepted patients with serious criminal records. I responded in the affirmative, adding by way of a condition that all applicants had to pass an assessment prior to admission. Approximately an hour later the mystery deepened when a Mr. Rawlings, an executive from Social Services, rang to say I would be receiving a referral from a CPN (Community Psychiatric Nurse). It would be in respect of a category 'A' prisoner who had been released after serving his sentence less the time off given for good behaviour some months previously.

'Would you be kind enough to tell me the nature of his crime?' I asked reasonably.

'I'm sorry but I cannot divulge that.' The voice was firm and unfriendly.

'Well I'm extremely sorry, but I shall not be assessing him then.' The receiver went dead, I replaced mine thoughtfully.

The following day shortly after lunch, he rang again. 'Ms. de Villiers you are an extremely arrogant woman.' I pondered for a moment on how he could have possibly come to such a conclusion having spoken to me for less than a minute during which time I spoke only twenty five words.

'You are not improving your chances of an admission for your client by insulting me.' My reply was defiant, but not aggressively presumptuous.

'Look! Could we call a truce?' His voice had softened, I detected a note of desperation.

'You started the war,' I said.

'Yes but it's a stressful situation and I want the best for my client and your project is the best. I apologise for what I said.'

'I will accept your apology on one condition, and that is you stop telling lies and cease to patronise either me or my clinic. You have applied to me because no-one else will accept your client and if you don't get him placed he will have to go back to prison, am I correct?'

There was a silence, much longer than would be normally expected and I wanted to enquire if he was still there, but I did not. It was not my intention for him to think I was interested one way or the other.

'You are very perceptive Ms de Villiers.' His tone was resigned.

'Perceptive and arrogant! You must do something about your stress factor, Mr. Rawlings.' And before he could reply. 'What was his crime?'

'He committed, was subsequently found guilty and sentenced for the Ealing Vicarage rape.' Now it was my turn to be silent, stuck for words that would offer a prompt reply, now it was Mr. Rawlings who wanted to know if we were still connected. His enquiry was brisk. This time my reply immediate.

'Yes, you can bring him for assessment either Wednesday or Thursday twenty-first or twenty-second at two p.m.'

Rawlings promised to pass the appointment availabilities on to the CPN and must have done so quite quickly, because she confirmed Thursday the twenty- second within the hour.

I recall not sleeping much that night, tossing and turning hour after hour, getting up at least half a dozen times and drinking far too much coffee. I imagined the ordeal Jill Saward had suffered at the hands of her aggressors, recalled with little difficulty the torment of similar anguish in my own existence and when my eyes did close, it was only to endure vivid highly technicolour images of an hallucinatory nature. It was me not her they were raping.

I was familiar with the criminal fraternity. A

184

significant proportion of our client group had been imprisoned at some stage or another for crimes committed while under the influence of drink and drugs, or for obtaining money by deception to feed their habits. More than one resembled the average person in the street's perception of a mass murderer - built like brick out-houses, shaven heads, tattoos in profusion and a distinctly threatening persona. There was more than one standard joke about me at work, referring to ex-cons trembling with trepidation when the clinic tannoy boomed out the request they attend my office at once. One stands out: 'What's the difference between a three year stretch and a bollocking from Nikki?' Answer - 'The three stretch goes quicker.' I was amused, and I'm not ashamed to say inwardly proud: my credibility had been hard earned.

'Your appointment has arrived Nikki.' Billy's voice over the internal telephone link was matter-of-fact but businesslike. He had been particularly difficult to train. With only one tooth remaining in what should have been the upper set, and a certain degree of mental disturbance created by too many heavy sessions, he was prone to forget just about everything of any consequence, unless it was connected to motor cycles or Arsenal Football Club. On the occasions when memory loss prevailed, he simply made things up as he went along often with catastrophic results. Chastisement was followed with a one-tooth grin which raised my hackles so high he was in danger of being impaled. When finally I persuaded him to have the rest of his decayed fangs removed and a false set fitted, I was usually greeted with a gummy grin while he simultaneously rummaged around in his pocket looking for the false set. I've known them turn up in the house laundry, drug trolley and at least once in a Health Authority skip. Success was now mine; today he was immaculate in clinic uniform - and a complete set.

'Mr. Dunning (pseudonym) to see you Nikki.' I paused for a moment...then. 'Put him in the Magnolia Room please Billy.'

Jonathan Dunning cowered in the corner of the assessment room, crying softly and shaking almost rhythmically; the room, as nearly always at times like this, stank of stale alcohol. I asked a couple of irrelevant questions which allowed me to concentrate on studying him closely, my imagination running wild, rooted in terrors I had personally endured. I pondered on how many more females like me had suffered the same fate as Jill Saward but were afraid to report the assaults, or alternatively lacked the circumstances that would scream out from newspaper headlines guaranteeing public sympathy. This did not detract from Jill Saward's courage or her misery, however it did raise the question of whether law and order responded more readily to where obvious innocence and compassion was a galvanizing force. The police throughout my ordeal in the aftermath of the rape by my father acted with callous indifference, and one officer positively enjoyed asking certain questions and my answers even more. The chances of them pulling off a successful prosecution in my case were negligible, thus I was undoubtedly discriminated against on a needs to win basis. This raises the serious issue of how many other females receive similar treatment to me and succumb to signing a retraction. Although it has to be said that after the Ealing Vicarage rape during the middle to late eighties, the whole question of police handling of rape victims was altered radically.

The very last thing I desire would be to attempt to lessen blame or even one degree of responsibility for the Ealing crime. I am a woman, who has suffered, as previously described, rape by my father and at the hands of others on too many occasions. Time has mellowed my anger, brought peace to my soul and all but eradicated any form of resentment. It was probably due to this unfathomable conversion, that I aspired to look into the personification of this man who is described, alongside his partners, as guilty of one of the most outrageous crimes of the twentieth century. I had been involved in the mopping up process, so it was with professional and personal interest I noted through the television news that Jill Saward, an incredibly forgiving and compassionate lady, was leading the way by agreeing to meet one of her tormentors who wished to offer an apology face to face. I was impressed.

For my part, I called upon a personal inner strength from I know not where, in order to arrange an individualistic therapy plan for

Jonathan Dunning where he received a just and proper unbiased treatment programme from myself and trusted colleagues. However, I shall never forget returning to the sanctuary of my office after the initial interview and breaking out in a cold sweat during which my whole body shook involuntarily and I burst into floods of tears. I had just faced symbolically and simultaneously every man who had ever abused me in my entire life. I was thinking in terms of my two hundred plus such violations and suddenly felt aware of the hideousness of my experiences. I had attracted so much abuse simply as a result of regularly 'drinking to forget' to the point where I had lost everything and needed food and somewhere to sleep. It came at an horrendous price.

Part of my assessment at the six week stage of his treatment makes interesting reading:-

'Jonathan is talking a lot of sense and I only hope he means what he says. He appears a straight talking guy now he is completely sober and is quite likeable.'

Paradoxically, I find it perverse to align this description to a man who committed a most heinous crime. Such is the power of alcohol.

My attention was drawn back to the hotel television set. My thoughts ran deep. Jill Saward's compassion persuaded me to go and face my father, ask him why, and offer forgiveness. Two days later my mother telephoned to say he was dead.

CHAPTER TWENTY-TWO

COMPROMISE

My intention was the early night would include sleep, but it was not to be. I lay tossing and turning and finally rang the night porter to enquire into the possibility of a pot of tea. He was a charming man who had kindly added a plate of biscuits to the tray he delivered whilst telling me he had a daughter my age. I sat up in bed munching shortcakes, drinking tea and thinking over my stay, silently acknowledging it had been successful by and large and decided to summarise the outcome of it all.

On reflection I realised I had not recovered from my illness and knew I never would. I had found a way with Justin's help, of negotiating life that was acceptable and provided me with a degree of happiness that, although flawed, was tolerable at worst and satisfactory at best. There were moments when I was happy to the point of exhilaration when those around me were lifted too, such was the power of my personality. I reverted back in minutes, and was devastated when I saw those whom I loved react with disappointment because the happiness so recently witnessed was not permanent after all.

Despite having survived many years without alcohol or drugs of any sort and learned to trust a small group of people unconditionally. I still occasionally scratch myself superficially but painfully, in places no-one ever sees, because deep down I believe I deserve to suffer. In much the same way as a former cigarette smoker may keep an unopened packet in a secret place, there is always a Wilkinson Sword razor blade in my handbag. It somehow gives me an unfathomable and indescribable sense of security, that should I decide I need punishment, the means will always be there.

I dislike the human race, and could count those I trust on the fingers of one hand. The people I thought wonderful in my childhood, whose love and devotion I never questioned, destroyed my life as surely as if they had shot me dead. My misery began when reality finally registered at the age of twelve that they were not what I thought they were - the years until I reached thirty were purgatory personified. I was not complaining for myself, neither was I wallowing in self pity, I was merely summarising as part of my journey of remembrance, exactly where my treatment and subsequent life had led me.

My work has convinced me that the sexual abuse of children is an epidemic running totally out of control. Those not involved have not the vaguest conception of what it entails, how it is executed, or how it is often incredibly well organized with military style precision. The ogres responsible are deluded into believing what they do is acceptable, because the victims seem to enjoy it when in reality they know no different. Those who abused me during the rest of my life were enabled to do so as a result of damage perpetrated upon me in my childhood, while they themselves or I were under the influence of alcohol and/or drugs. I was inexorably drawn to those capable of abuse and their kind as mysteriously and devastatingly as a moth to a flame.

I took a deep breath and slumped back deeply into the pillow suddenly aware I had spoken some of my thoughts aloud. Inexplicably I felt a satisfaction in my conclusions and I knew it was time to go home.

CHAPTER TWENTY-THREE
FAREWELL

I awoke, with the sun predictably streaming through my hotel bedroom window and Justin in my mind's eye!

I packed my single suitcase carefully, took a last look around the room, under the bed and through every drawer, then closing the door gently behind me took the lift to reception.

'Ms. de Villiers you're leaving us today, have you enjoyed your stay?' I nodded, smiled simultaneously and asked if there was somewhere I could leave the case while I did a little shopping. 'Yes of course, leave it here behind the counter and the porter will put it into the room provided.' I double checked the car would be O.K to leave in the hotel's underground car park and then headed for town. I walked slowly and deliberately, concentrating on how privileged I was to have been delivered safely from the horror and repugnance of my life. My stay had been a voyage of enlightenment in so many ways and as Justin had promised, there were no evil spirits or demonic fiends waiting to grab me on every street corner. The few people I had met were charming and pleased to see me, there had been laughter, much reminiscing and of course an enigma.

Sainsbury's was my final port of call, but first I went to W.H.Smith and carefully selected a small, expensive Bible with a beautiful white cover, exactly the same as the one Miss Lewis had given me at the railway station all those years ago, and which I treasure to the present day. I sat on a bench in the Abbey churchyard which I now amusingly thought of as my own, opened it gently and wrote on a plain page...

> **To Hayley**
> **Have a happy life**
> **Love from Nikki**
>   **xx**

I closed it gently, placed it back in the bag provided and walked to Sainsbury's.

I went into the store and pretended to browse for a while because I could not see the reason for my visit. I was about to give up and leave when suddenly I saw her enter from the 'staff only' area at the rear of the store. She was accompanied by a girl around her own age whom I recognised from a previous visit, she had an arm around Hayley who had obviously been crying. They were probably returning from a coffee break and I continued my shopping pretext, all the time moving more closely to where she had resumed the tedious job of stacking shelves.

'Hello, how nice to see you again,' she said. I swung around pretending to look surprised and noticed she was trying hard to smile through a blotchy tear stained face. 'I've just popped in to buy a few things before I return to London.' I said. I moved towards her pretending to look more closely into her face and then spoke again. 'You've been crying, are you unhappy?'

'I've been having trouble at home,' she spoke quietly but continued, 'I'm going to leave and find a place of my own.' 'Don't do that.' I said too quickly, she looked up surprised at my outburst. 'I'm sorry,' I added almost at once, 'I have no right to interfere, but when I was your age I did something similar which I've regretted all my life. You're much too nice to suffer like I have over a silly mistake you may live to regret forever. Has something gone terribly wrong at home?' My words seemed to run together as I had spoken without taking a breath.

'It's just that...my parents don't approve of my boyfriend.' I looked at her quizzically.

'It's because he's still married to someone else, but it's me he loves.' Now it was she who spoke too hurriedly.

'Have you considered they might be right? You're very young you know and I can't help but think you deserve something better than second best.'

'What on earth do you mean?' Her eyes were flashing, hands on hips.

'Well, you're such a sweet girl, and he is second hand isn't he? I think you deserve someone of your very, very own, someone new.'

She looked at me with mouth open, then closed, then open again. 'You grown-ups are all the same,' she said finally.

'It's because we used to be children once and we have learned, in some cases, terrible lessons we want to pass on to those we care about.' I said slowly. 'Look, I hope you don't mind but I have bought you something, because when we spoke the other day you reminded me of someone who was once very close to me. You probably think I'm a silly old woman and perhaps I am, but I would like you to have it.' I put the bag containing the white jacketed Bible into her hand. 'Don't open it now,' I said softly, then added. 'Please think again before you make your decision.' I turned and hurried from the store.

I was glad to be outside breathing the warm summer air and did so deeply. It made me feel a little heady and my heart was beating faster than it normally did, but I felt happier and more at peace than I had for a very long time.

Abruptly I heard a voice - 'Hey! wait a minute, please stop.' I turned around, it was Hayley running towards me. She was quite breathless by the time she reached my side and spoke while gulping for air.

'I'm really sorry if I was unkind to you.' she gasped. 'I read what you put, but my name's Sally. I remind you of someone called Hayley don't I?' I nodded.

195

'I hope you'll have a happy life too,' she said. 'And do you want to know something else?' I had half turned to walk away. 'Of course,' I said. 'I think you're right,' she announced. 'My parents are not bad really, they've done lots of nice kind things for me over the years and have always given me the best they can afford.' She looked down at the ground momentarily.

'Yes,' I said. 'And one day when you are my age you will think of those things when they're no longer here, and you will be so glad you made the right decision. Always remember you deserve better than second best.'

'That's a lovely thing to say.' Hayley who was Sally spoke haltingly swallowing hard. 'Goodbye,' she said. 'Goodbye,' I whispered.

Hayley turned away ... I turned the page and felt so proud that commonsense and wisdom had come out of my instability. The enigma remained. There were many loose ends, but the sun was shining and a weight was removed.

... Hayley had survived of that I was quite certain - I simply did not want to know definitively.

A change of colour had taken place in the lining of my cloud.

A phrase from the lips of my beloved Miss Lewis entered my mind - I spoke it aloud....

'Thy will be done.'

The moving finger writes; and, having writ,
Moves on: nor all thy piety nor wit
Shall lure it back to cancel half a line,
Nor all thy tears wash out a word of it.

The Rubaiyat of Omar Khayyam

Edward Fitzgerald